J·M·BARRIE
..and the..
THEATRE

SIR J. M. BARRIE, Bart., O.M.

From a Photo
by G. C. Beresford.

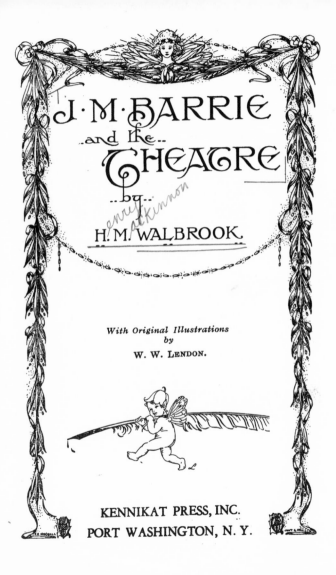

J·M·BARRIE
and the
THEATRE
by
H. M. WALBROOK

With Original Illustrations
by
W. W. LENDON.

KENNIKAT PRESS, INC.
PORT WASHINGTON, N. Y.

TO MY WIFE.

J. M. BARRIE AND THE THEATRE

First published 1922
Reissued 1969 by Kennikat Press

Library of Congress Catalog Card No: 68-8215
Manufactured in the United States of America

Contents.

5

6 Contents *(continued)*.

List of Illustrations.

" Losh, losh, but it's a queer warld ! "

J. M. BARRIE

AND

THE THEATRE.

SINCE 1902, the year of the production of *The Admirable Crichton*, Sir J. M. Barrie has been one of the most interesting figures in the British Theatre. No other dramatist has given so much delight to so many people and at the same time lived so apart from public life. The newspaper " interviewer " has long regarded him as morbidly elusive, nor has the most determined roar of " Author ! " yet succeeded in drawing him into the glare of the footlights. He has probably never made a public speech which has not been " the speech of the evening," yet the number of his efforts in this direction could very likely be counted on the fingers of one hand. Of self-advertisement, much less self-glorification, he has never shown the smallest sign. When, late in the day, he consented to edit a printed edition of his plays, he confined his commentary strictly to the plays and their characters, and gave us none of those fascinating accounts of their origins such as Sir W. S. Gilbert condescended to supply to certain printed editions of his opera libretti, and even Henry James, in all too small a measure, contributed to a " definitive " edition of his novels and stories.

A reserved man, troubling himself little about society, taking a modest part in conversation, but when pleased with a neighbour's remark, turning suddenly, looking him full in the face, and laughing like a boy —Sir J. M. Barrie has yet found honours fall thick upon him. Born on May 9th, 1860, at Kirriemuir, in Forfarshire, and educated at Dumfries Academy and Edinburgh University, he was awarded the honorary degree of LL.D. by his University in 1909, made a baronet in 1913, elected Rector of

St. Andrews University in 1919, and awarded the Order of Merit in 1922. Only three other men have been awarded this last honour solely as men of Letters : George Meredith, Henry James, and Thomas Hardy. These distinctions, moreover, have been conferred upon him amid an ever-growing chorus of popular approval. The *Times* put the general feeling regarding him into a sentence the day the conferment upon him of the Order of Merit was announced : " Thousands have been charmed, charmed, charmed to tears, to laughter, to terror, to adoration, by the infinitely various cleverness with which he reveals his lovableness."

Sir J. M. Barrie has made the village of Kirriemuir famous throughout the English-speaking world as " Thrums," but London has been the scene and centre of most of his triumphs. He was beckoned from Nottingham to the great city by one of the ablest and noblest figures in English journalism, Frederick Greenwood, the founder and first editor of the *Pall Mall Gazette* and the *St. James's Gazette ;* and his first article in the latter journal appeared on November 17th, 1884, and was called " An Auld Licht

Community." Occupying a column and a quarter in that very charming evening paper, it described an Auld Licht kirk and congregation, and was rich in such humorous touches as that of the precentor, Lang Tammas, who never but once had an altercation with his minister, and that was when he put half-a-crown by mistake into the kirk plate, and insisted on having two-and-fivepence back or changing his denomination.

Two other distinguished editors who recognised and encouraged his genius in those early days were William Ernest Henley, the poet and critic, who was also the editor of the *National Observer*, the most brilliant weekly paper of its day ; and Sir William Robertson Nicoll, the editor of the *British Weekly*. To these three good friends he has, we know, ever been grateful, and particularly, of course, to Mr. Greenwood. On April 8th, 1905, a complimentary dinner was given to that great journalist at the Trocadero, presided over by Mr. John Morley, M.P. (afterwards Viscount Morley of Blackburn), and attended by most of the leading writers of the day. Mr. Barrie (as he then was) had been the chairman of the organising committee, and towards the end of the evening he had to respond to the toast of "The Committee." In doing so he made what Sir W. Robertson Nicoll afterwards described as a speech which no one who heard it would ever forget. Scraps of it have survived to these latter days: "However much the other members of the committee may love Mr. Greenwood, I love him more, for he invented me." . . . "I owe him almost everything" . . "I bought my first silk hat when I came to London solely to impress him. In his honour we now take off every hat we have, but it was those first silk hats that meant the most. Old and battered are they now, but even they rise again and salute Mr. Greenwood." In his attractive volume, "A Bookman's Letters," Sir William Robertson Nicoll says: "Of all the young writers whom Frederick Greenwood made famous, he regarded with the greatest love and pride J. M. Barrie."

Another of our dramatist's early admirers and friends was George Meredith, who, writing to Greenwood concerning his election in 1890 to membership of the Garrick Club, said: "Barrie's election honours the club." Yet another was his countryman, Robert

Louis Stevenson, who wrote of him to Henry James in December, 1892 : " Barrie is a beauty. Stuff in that young man, but he must see and not be too funny. Genius in him, but there's a journalist at his elbow— there's the risk." In the same month he wrote to Barrie himself : " I am proud to think you are a Scotchman." I will venture to say that if Stevenson had lived to see *Mary Rose* he would joyfully have acknowledged that the " journalist at his elbow " had not done his friend much harm.

Apart from the patriotism of honest work done to the best of his ability—and, after all, that is not such a bad form of patriotism—Sir J. M. Barrie has served his country in other and equally important ways. During the great war he not only helped the Red Cross and other patriotic organisations with his pen and his personal influence, but fulfilled a particularly valuable function in interpreting the cause of Britain to the people of the United States at a time when certain other interpreters were busying themselves exceedingly on the other side of the Atlantic. In the February of 1919, when his comedy, *Dear Brutus*, was being acted at the Empire Theatre, New York,

he sent the following letter to the actor,
Mr. W. Gillette, who read it to the audience :—

> *Dear Brutus* is an allegory about a
> gentleman called John Bull, who, years and
> years ago, missed the opportunity of his life.
> The ' Mr. Dearth' of the play is really John Bull.
> The play shows how on the fields of France
> father and daughter get a second opportunity.
> Are now the two to make it up permanently,
> or for ever drift apart ? A second chance
> comes to few. As for a third chance, who ever
> heard of it ? It's now or never. If it is now,
> something will have been accomplished greater
> than war itself. Future mankinds are listening
> for our decision. If we cannot rise to this
> second chance ours will be the blame, but the
> sorrow will be posterity's.

His writings, whether novels or plays, have
been as popular in America as at home, and
this letter came straight from his heart. It
was both written and received as the letter
of a friend to friends.

For the rest, our author would probably
insist that his most illustrious days have
been those on which he has played cricket
at Lord's. It is darkly whispered that both
there and elsewhere his pipe has generally
been still alight on his return, bat in hand,
from the wicket. If so, all one can say is
that he is not the only eminent lover of

cricket who has found similar consolation. One thing is certain : the fact that Sir J. M. Barrie's first comedy had a county cricketer for its hero and a budding one for its " juvenile comedy " was as characteristic of him as anything he has ever written.

And now—let us ring up the curtain !

CHAPTER I.

An Ibsen Burlesque.

SIR J. M. BARRIE started his career as a dramatist in the early summer of 1891 with a burlesque. The Ibsen drama was at that time dividing the serious side of playgoing London into two camps, (1) the "Ibsenites," led by Mr. William Archer, and (2) the active detesters of the Norwegian and all his works, led by Mr. Clement Scott, the critic of the theatre for the *Daily Telegraph*, who had gone so far as to classify the Ibsen drama as "Ibsene." The first of Ibsen's plays to stir the waters of theatrical

London had been " Et Dukkehjem " (" A
Doll's House "), produced at the Novelty
Theatre in 1889, with Miss Janet Achurch,
an actress of genius and striking personality,
in the character of Nora Helmer. No play
in contemporary European drama had at
once so delighted and so offended the diverse
tastes of the intellectual world as this picture of a cosy household wrecked in the
first place by a doting husband, and in the
second by a devoted wife and mother. One
school of critics hailed the famous shutting
of the door at the end of the last Act as a
sort of commemorative and glorious dis-
charge of the guns of Freedom. The other
raged against it as a repulsive *feu de joie* over
the grave of all Decency and Respectability.

After " A Doll's House " came " Hedda
Gabler," translated into English by Mr.
Edmund Gosse, and produced at the Vaudeville on April 20th, 1891, by two enthusiastic
young actresses, Miss Elizabeth Robins
and Miss Marion Lea, for a modest " five
consecutive matinées." It was said at the
time that, in order to defray the initial
expenses of the production, the two young
actresses had valiantly pawned their jewels,
and, in a world of materialism, one liked to

believe the story, particularly as the production proved so attractive that the
originally planned five matinées developed
into several weeks of afternoon and evening
representations. The performance was,
indeed, one of the finest of its day. No other
acting so subtle was to be seen in a modern
play in London, and crowded audiences
followed each of the four long Acts in a still-
ness so profound that it resembled that of a
church rather than that of a playhouse.
The Press, however, gave it a very poor
reception. Even the *Times* could say little
more for the play than that it was "a
demonstration of the pathology of mind
such as may be found in the *Journal of
Mental Science*, or in the reports of the
medical superintendents of lunatic asylums,"
and added the following mournful fore-
bodings :—

> To conceive of the Ibsen Drama gaining an
> extensive or permanent foothold on the stage
> is hardly possible. Playgoing would then
> cease to be an amusement and become a
> penance, and the function of the dramatist
> in society would be similar to that of the
> skeleton at the Egyptian feast.

It is almost as dangerous to prophesy on the

theatre as on cricket. More than thirty years have passed since that was written, and we all know that Ibsen's plays have gained a permanent and even an extensive foothold on the European and American stage; that the theatre is still a popular source of recreation in all civilised countries; and that " the function of the dramatist in society " (whatever that phrase may have been intended to mean) is still on the whole an exceedingly cheerful one.

The cast of the memorable Vaudeville production of " Hedda Gabler " deserves to be set down here. It was as follows :—

George Tesman (a young man of letters)
                                    Mr. Scott Buist
Mrs. Hedda Tesman (*née* Gabler, his wife)
                                    Miss Elizabeth Robins
Miss Juliana Tesman (his aunt)
                                    Miss Henrietta Cowen
Mrs. Elvsted ...   ...   Miss Marion Lea
Judge Brock   ... Mr. Charles Sugden
Ejlert Lövborg   ...   Mr. A. Elwood
Bertha (servant to the Tesmans)
                                    Miss Patty Chapman

It is often said that the art of the player dies with the fall of the curtain upon him. It may be so, but I know that at this moment, more than thirty years after, I can

see the glare of Miss Robins and hear her
malevolent cries of satisfaction as she
crammed Lövborg's manuscript into the
stove at the end of the third Act, still hear
the musical tones and slow speech of Arthur
Elwood in the character of the doomed
young historian, and see the wistful, delicate
beauty of Miss Lea in the character of his
scarcely less ill-fated " comrade," Théa
Elvsted. Such revelations of art and of
personality as these players gave us in this
performance have a long life in memory
and a longer one still in history.

Such was the event which moved Barrie
to write his first produced dramatic composition, a piece which, although it only
occupied about half an hour in performance, raised more laughter in Toole's
Theatre than many a three-act farce had
evoked. He entitled it *Ibsen's Ghost, or
Toole up-to-date*, and his name did not
appear on the programme at the first performance. It was acted for the first time
on Saturday afternoon, May 31st, 1891, the
day on which that year's official celebration
of the Queen's birthday took place. The
day turned out to be so wet and foggy that
the ceremony of the Trooping of the Colour

had to be abandoned. It was, indeed, just the day for dropping into a warm, cheerful, brightly-lighted little theatre and having a good laugh, and our author's diverting " Hedda in one Act," as he classified his invention, provided for that quite brilliantly.

There is no need to tell here the story of the original drama. The book is, or should be, on the shelves of every serious student of the modern European Theatre. All I need mention is that the burlesque carries it several stages further. When the curtain rises on *Ibsen's Ghost*, Théa Elvsted has for some time been George Tesman's second wife, and the inevitable Ibsenite separation is at hand. We find her burning her love-letters in the famous stove. She has developed a fatal and uncontrollable habit of kissing every man she meets. " This morning I kissed three," she moans, " all of them strange men to me ! " and her poor husband can only explain, " Fancy that ! " It turns out that this habit of indiscriminate kissing is a mania inherited from her grandfather, who, on the eve of her wedding had kissed one of her prettiest bridesmaids in the dark, and has been kissing other girls ever since. In the end this unhappy wife, like her predecessor, commits suicide. Poor Hedda had slain herself with one of her father's pistols. Barrie's Théa put an end to her troubles with a child's popgun.

One of the queer touches in the burlesque was the fact that the futile and spectacled Tesman was for ever mixing up Théa with Hedda, and addressing his second wife by the name of his first, much to her resentment. There was a scene in which he was sitting at a table at the back of the room writing a review of a large new volume that lay before him, and obviously worried over the task. Presently his wife drifted weirdly in, and stood gazing mournfully at him as he sat running desperate fingers through his hair. Suddenly he looked up and caught sight of her, and the following conversation ensued :—

> TESMAN : Hedda, dear——
> THEA (*weirdly*) : I am not Hedda. I am Théa.
> TESMAN : I beg pardon. Is there a " k " in " Christianity " ?
> THEA (*very weirdly and slowly*) : There—is— nothing—in Christianity.
> TESMAN : Fancy that !

The part of Tesman was played with rich

drollery by the admirable comedian who was afterwards to do much other entertaining work in the Barrie drama, Mr. George Shelton, while the Théa was Miss Irene Vanbrugh, then a young actress quite unknown to the general public, but already exhibiting the brilliant personality and admirable art destined later to make her a leading figure of the English stage. Miss Vanbrugh's imitation of the mystical tones and glances of Miss Marion Lea was one of the subtlest and most diverting pieces of mimicry I have ever seen. The part of the genial and disreputable old grandfather was played by the famous comedian, Mr. J. L. Toole, made-up with bushy whiskers to look like Ibsen ; and Miss Eliza Johnstone was equally droll as the elderly " Doll's House " wife, who reproached her husband for having never brought home disreputable characters, and tearfully upbraided him for standing by and allowing her children to call her " Mother."

In those days Burlesque was a standing dish in the London theatrical world, the Gaiety being its principal temple, and Mr. Edward Terry its leading exponent. Many of the leading Grand Operas of the day were burlesqued in the most amusing way, and playgoers who saw " Little Doctor Faust," " Young Fra Diavolo," " Robbing Roy," " The Bohemian Gyurl," and many other equally agreeable irreverences remembered them for years among their most joyous hours. Even Shakespeare's tragedies were not immune, and a burlesque of " Hamlet," in which Mr. Terry impersonated the Ghost in Roman armour and a short black beard, and cracked jokes at the expense of Mr. Wilson Barrett, whose flamboyant impersonation of the Danish prince was at that time being given at the Princess's, evoked great laughter. Years after, in the course of a walk over the Downs near Brighton, I asked Mr. Terry why he had given up acting in Burlesque, and his answer was : " Because the actors and actresses of the present day do not know how to speak the puns." Anyone who had heard Mr. Terry deliver one of these verbal contortions, such, for example, as

O what a noise ! O what a horrid shindy !
Those Ethiopians *'neath-the-opian* windy !

dragging it up, as it were, from the bowels of the earth, could easily believe that the art of it was by no means a simple one.

Ibsen's Ghost drew many people to the little theatre in King William Street (on the site of which the Charing Cross Eye Hospital was afterwards built) who had never visited it before. The skit was never revived, and I believe the only text published of it was a German one, printed in Germany. Mr. Toole's personal knowledge of Ibsen and his writings was peculiar rather than extensive. He never saw one of his plays acted, and in conversation would dismiss both the dramatist and his works as " horrid," and change the subject.

This amusing skit prepared the way for the longer piece that was to follow it in a few months, and was destined to make its author as well-known in the world of the footlights as he already was in that of the novel, the delightful farce in three Acts, *Walker, London.*

CHAPTER II.

J. L. TOOLE AND THE CUCKOO.

TOOLE'S Theatre in those days was
regarded as a temple of Laughter
rather than as one of Art. Its actor-
manager was one of the most popular figures
in the theatrical world, both personally
and as a player, but it was not equally easy
to all playgoers to enjoy his performances.
The principal reason for this was the old-
fashioned character of most of his favourite
parts and of the plays in which they were
set. The comedy " Paul Pry," in which

he gave one of his most popular impersonations, was not half a century old in 1892,
yet how terribly it seemed to " date " and
how ancient appeared its talk and general
technique ! Even H. J. Byron's " Upper
Crust," for all its amusing lines, seemed
very *vieux jeu* to many of us, while such
pieces as " The Spitalfields Weaver " and
" Dot " impressed one as antiquity itself.
The comedian suffered considerably from
having to appear in these mechanical com-
positions. He was compelled to force the
note of comicality, to over-emphasise a
comic line or a comic situation in tone,
gesture and facial play. Hence the sense of
shock and of wondering relief when he
produced on his tiny stage a pièce so agree-
ably modern as *Ibsen's Ghost.* And this
pleasant emotion was intensified a hundred-
fold when, on Thursday evening, February
25th, 1892, the three-act comic play,
Walker, London, was given for the first time.

A few days before, another dramatist
had enjoyed a triumphal " first appearance "
at the St. James's Theatre, Mr. Oscar Wilde,
the author of " Lady Windermere's Fan,"
and the town was still laughing over the
scene which had taken place when at the

close of that first performance the author, smoking a cigarette, appeared upon the stage and assured the audience that he had spent a thoroughly enjoyable evening. At the end of the third Act of *Walker, London*, there was also great applause, and when the actors and actresses had bowed their acknowledgments, cries of " Author !" rose from all parts of the house. For a long time they continued, but no author appeared, and at last Mr. Toole stepped upon the stage alone, and, raising his hand to beget silence, proceeded to inform the audience that he had to apologise on three grounds for Mr. Barrie's absence. The three grounds were :—

1. He is too nervous to appear.
2. He is not in the theatre.
3. He does not smoke !

This last produced perhaps the loudest laugh of the whole evening. As a sly dig at Mr. Wilde it was enjoyed by everybody ; and as a description of a gentleman who was known to be extremely devoted to his pipe, and even to a certain tobacco, it gave quite exquisite pleasure to those of his personal friends who were present

Walker, London, is one of the lightest of farces. It is not a classic like " The Importance of Being Earnest," a piece which in its combination of wit, humour, neat construction, and literary polish, stands alone in the modern British comic theatre. *Walker, London,* belongs rather to the Tom Robertson class of comedy. Its fun is largely domestic and it is full of sentiment. It offers us two pairs of lovers, and they are both the nice, old-fashioned, adoring sort of lovers that any audience is certain to take to its heart at once. In the first Act, it is true, one of the adored and adoring young ladies, Miss Bell Golightly, a graduate of Girton, declares solemnly to her worshipper, Mr. Kit Upjohn, the county cricketer, that their love must be reasonable and intellectual, and not disfigured by the abject silliness of lovers in general. When he (who by no means shares these views) kisses her and calls her " My beautiful ! " she pours forth the following flood of eloquence upon him :—

> You must never pay me thése infantile compliments to my personal appearance. If you love me, let it be for my mind alone, for all other love is founded on an ontological

misconception. I must be your helpmate in all things. Should I seem unreasonable you must never humour me. No laughing me out of my arguments, nor kissing away my judgment ! You will never yield to me for that most despicable of all reasons, because you think me pretty.

But in the third Act this very young lady collapses as badly into sentimental babyism as any happy maiden of Balham or Tooting. Resting her head on the broad bosom of her champion cricketer, she even whispers at his bidding the words, " D- -n Logic !" and when he, taking her head in his hands and speaking with great solemnity says, " Does oo love me, 'ickle pet ?" she nestles closely to him and as solemnly answers, " 'Ess, me does love oo. Does oo love *me* ?" The acting of these scenes at Toole's Theatre by such charming young players as Miss Irene Vanbrugh and Mr. Charles Lowne was so amusing that one could enjoy it again and again.

The scene of the comedy is a house-boat on the Thames by Clevedon Woods, near Maidenhead, and its chief character is a humble London hairdresser named Jasper Phipps, who was to have married a worthy spinster of his own class, one Sarah Rigg, but has run away from her on the wedding morning, taking the honeymoon money with him and sending her the following letter :—

> "My dearest Sarah, You will be surprised at my not turning up to marry you, and I feel I owe you an apology. First, my love, it is a startler to a man to wake up on his marriage morning and remember that in an hour he will be tied up for life. Second, through shaving so many gents, I feel that I want to have a burst as one myself. Sarah, it can only be done with the honeymoon money. Third, my sweet, I know a swell I'm like in appearance, and I am going to pass for him, but he is a bachelor, so it wouldn't be proper to take you with me. Fourth, it would be more difficult for you than for me to look like a swell. Fifth, there is not enough money for two at any rate. Everything considered, dear Sarah, I have decided to have the honeymoon before the marriage, and to have it by myself. Then, my girl, when my week's leave is up, I will come back and marry you. Fear not, I am staunch. And don't follow me.
>
>   Your affectionate JASPER.
>   P.S.—I love you! I love you! I love you!"

And, wandering placidly along by the river, this worthy suddenly sees a beautiful young lady fall into the stream. As it happens

she has only tumbled into two feet of water,
and a passing boatman, one Ben, pulls her
out with a boat-hook, drenched and temporarily unconscious, having fainted from
the shock.   So Phipps, on the look-out for
adventure, bribes Ben with fifteen shillings
to tell everybody that he has been the
heroic rescuer.   When the damsel recovers
consciousness she naturally asks the name of
her valiant deliverer, and Phipps at once
replies that he is no less a person than the
renowned African explorer, Colonel Neil,
known as Africanus Neil ; whereupon the
young lady (who by the way is Miss Bell
Golightly, the champion of the Intellectual
in love) conducts him to the house-boat,
where her mother, brother and a number
of friends are spending a spring-time holiday.
Here he is lionised to the top of his bent and
brags of his exploits amid breathless wonder.
He also indulges in fits of dizziness which
involve him in the need of feminine support.
As he murmurs to himself when alone,
" That dizziness has let me in for some good
things! I shall go on being dizzy."   In
fact, he has the time of his life.

He is ignorant and illiterate, and has to
employ all his cockney cunning to avoid

" giving himself away " in answering the questions of his newly-found friends as to his adventures in Africa. When he hears one of the ladies speak of having visited the Alhambra in Spain, he inwardly concludes that it must be a music-hall similar to the one he knows in Leicester Square, and exclaims in an aside : " Fancy 'er being at the Alhambra, even though it *was* a Spanish one !'' Occasionally he lets his imagination run riot. Describing how he had killed an elephant in the African forest he adds, " An' when 'e lay dead 'ole troops of birds—eagles an' snipe, vultures, sparrows, canaries, turkeys, bull-rushes an' the oof bird*—all came flocking down on the corpse an' ate it up till there wasn't a bit left but the trunk, which I had made into a portmanteau !'' Now and then his invention fails him disastrously. " Did you see many mosquitoes in Africa, Colonel Neil ?'' asks one of the young ladies. " Mosquitoes ?'' replies the apostle of staunchness in a bewildered way, " Mosquitoes ?'' Then more self-confidently, " Oh, yes, thousands of 'em. Why, they were so tame they used to

*This allusion to "the oof bird" was probably a ' gag'' of Toole's.

come and eat out of my hand !"* In his
flirtation with the young ladies he strives
hard to be faithful to his Sarah. One of
them is Mrs. Golightly's niece, Nannie
O'Brien, a pretty young Irish girl, and she,
in her impulsive Irish way, pays him some
particularly agreeable compliments as they
sit close together side by side on the grassy
river bank. He feels called upon to make
an adequate emotional response, but does
not quite know how to set about it in the
case of a young lady so manifestly his social
superior. As he mutters to himself in
another aside: "I'd say to her, 'Nannie,
wilt thou gang with me ?' only I don't know
what 'gang' means !"

From time to time he hears a cuckoo
calling from among the trees, and the sound
stirs his conscience. He is for ever haunted
by the thought of his wronged and furious
Sarah, and by the fear of her tracking him
to his very pleasant hiding-place and
exposing him. In the scene with Nannie,
just referred to, he becomes conscious that
his fidelity to his homely betrothed in
London is in danger. "Look after me,

*This particular pleasantry was inserted by the
author for the 300th performance.

Sarah, I'm slipping!" he mutters to himself in a sort of prayer. And when at last
he can resist Nannie's tones and glances no
longer and kisses her, he immediately turns
his head away, and with an agonised
expression of countenance, gasps remorse-
fully to himself, " Sarah, I've slipped !"
Needless to say, Sarah does track him down,
and gets him away from his too fascinating
friends ; but he is able to hide her from
them and keep up his fraud to the end.
At the close of the play he has bidden them
a most affectionate farewell and pushes away
in a punt, while the party stand on the roof
of the house-boat waving their adieux to
the departing " Colonel." Suddenly they
remember that they have not his telegraphic
address, and one of them calls to him loudly
for it. For a few moments the only sound
heard is the gentle plash of the wavelets
among the sedges. Then a voice is heard
from the distance—the voice of the pseudo
explorer—and the address he proclaims
with a rich comic inflexion is " Walker,
London." On that the curtain falls.

As a rule, nothing is more dreadful as
literature than the " acting version " of a
play, with its innumerable directions to

actors and stage hands, but *Walker, London,*
is well worth reading even in this form.
Its technical construction is remarkably
sound. Indeed in this respect its author has
never surpassed it. In later plays he has,
of course, devised greater surprises, but they
have often arisen out of whimsicality, where-
as in *Walker, London* everything is built up
according to the familiar laws of dramatic
construction. It is, in short, a well-made
play of a quite old-fashioned kind, but rich
in wit and humour and brimming over with
high spirits. And it provided Mr. Toole
with a part in which all could enjoy him.
Many playgoers considered his Jasper Phipps
his best piece of work. His agonised groans
and facial contortions as he heard the
cuckoo calling and thought of his own un-
warrantable intrusion into the house-boat's
circle ; his moral collapses under the cold
eye of the blackmailing Ben ; his agonies
on the roof when he realised that Miss
Golightly had mistaken his philanderings
for a serious tender of affection, and his
twinges of remorse over the deserted Sarah
and the squandered honeymoon money, all
combined to make a figure of the richest
drollery.

The critics received the play with general applause. The writer of the review of it in the *Times* said a daring thing which has also proved a true one: " Like Rousseau, Mr. Barrie may flatter himself that as no one has anticipated him so he will have no imitator." Here, at any rate, a prophecy has been fulfilled, though the surprising thing is that a play so conventionally constructed as *Walker, London*, should have inspired it.

On the evening of the three hundredth performance a set of commemorative triolets appeared in *The Star*, then under the editorship of Mr. Ernest Parke, of which the last ran as follows :—

> So here's long life to Toole the Great,
>   And J.M. of the Barrie clan ;
> They've brought a playhouse up-to-date,
> So here's long life to Toole the Great !
>   And may good fortune ever wait
> On them and each true-hearted man !
> So here's long life to Toole the Great
>   And J.M. of the Barrie clan !

CHAPTER III.

A FAILURE AND A SUCCESS.

HAVING begun with a burlesque and continued with a farce, our dramatist now tried his hand at the book of words of a comic opera in collaboration with the inventor of Sherlock Holmes. At the Savoy Theatre, on the evening of May 13th, 1893, was presented for the first time the comic opera in two acts, *Jane Annie, or The Good Conduct Prize*, written by J. M. Barrie and Arthur Conan Doyle, and set to music by Ernest Ford. It was far from proving one of the events of the dramatic year as *Walker, London*, had done. It in no respect divided the honours with Irving's production

39

of Tennyson's " Becket " or Alexander's
production of Pinero's "The Second
Mrs. Tanqueray." In fact, *Jane Annie*
was an almost complete failure, and if its
prospects depended on the merits of its
" book " it deserved no other fate. To a
public familiar with the polished lyrics and
witty dialogue of W. S. Gilbert the libretto
of *Jane Annie* must have seemed the very
abomination of desolation. Those who remember the poem Sir J. M. Barrie wrote on
his friend after the death of Robert Louis
Stevenson will especially wonder at one
thing : there is not a poetical or witty lyric
in *Jane Annie* from beginning to end. Such
verses as

> Proctors have no acumen
> And no respect for women.

and

> School aristocratic,
> The scene most dramatic,
> Plot unsystematic
> And very erratic,

if not perhaps the world's worst are certainly among the old Savoy's worst. The
lyrics of *Jane Annie* never sing themselves
as Gilbert's do. And the plot is as bad as
the poetry In the second Act the story

makes an entirely fresh start, and even then the authors seem to find it difficult to spin it out to the required length. We find one of the characters indulging in such shameless padding as, " This discussion is getting hot. Perhaps I had better clear the air with a song," followed by half a page more talk about the ditty before it arrives. And when at last it does come it proves to be a thing of the feeblest point and humour. Nor is the character of the heroine much of a help to the piece. In the first Act Jane Annie is a sneak ; in the second she is openly and unattractively naughty, and always she is " unsympathetic."

There is a certain interest in reading the printed libretto to-day and trying to guess the pages that are by Barrie and those that are by Conan Doyle. One feels pretty sure that the queer idea of the marginal notes on the opera, supposed to be written by one of the characters in it, a golf caddie, came from Barrie. One of these *obiter dicta* is appended to the quatrain quoted above, and runs as follows :—

Grey and Sim (two " bulldogs ") have a bet that the critic will quote the third and fourth lines here, and say that they apply to the opera.

That reads like Barrie. And at the end of the first Act the heroine is revealed as endowed with hypnotising and mesmerising powers. Here one seems to " sense " the touch of that explorer in the occult, Sir A. Conan Doyle.

It is pleasant to turn from this unlucky effort to the evening of Monday, June 25th, 1894, when *The Professor's Love-Story*, which had already been produced in the United States with much success, was acted for the first time in London at the Comedy Theatre. That day had been an agitated one for the general public, for the morning papers had contained the announcements of two such events as the birth of the present Prince of Wales at White Lodge, Richmond, and the abominable assassination of M. Carnot, the deeply-respected President of the French Republic. Consequently, it was before an unusually excited audience that the curtain rose on the comedy that was to enjoy a run of hundreds of perform- ances and to move countless thousands of people to laughter and tears.

In *Walker, London*, the dramatist had brought the refreshing air of the upper river across the footlights. In *The Professor's Love-Story* he brought the " atmosphere " of Scottish rural life at harvest time across that remorseless frontier, just as MM. Erckmann-Chatrian had conveyed that of rural life in Alsace in some of the most charming of their plays. Its honeysuckle-laden cottages with their tell-tale lighted windows o' nights, its pleasant lanes, stooks of corn, trysting trees, and dryly cautious Scots labouring men, as canny in the affairs of love as in less sentimental matters, all created a most enjoyable illusion.

Fundamentally, the new comedy was incredibility itself. It called upon its audience to believe (1) That a Professor of Science in his 'forties might fall in love with his pretty young amanuensis and not possess the least idea of what has happened to him; (2) That he may be unable to work, sleep or think by reason of his passion, and yet feel helplessly constrained to consult a physician as to the reason for his symptoms; and (3) That on being told the nature of his seizure he may bewilderedly and indignantly ask, " But who is the woman ? " As the *Times* critic remarked, it did indeed need the subtlest art of the dramatist to

save such incidents from " wearing the
guise of puerilities." And I am not sure
if even these assaults upon the common-
sense of the public were not surpassed
when the dramatist made a learned
physician mistake the phrase " cherchez la
femme " for the name of a new disease !*

In spite of all this extravagance, however, the success of the dramatist was complete. Not the first audience only but more
than five hundred succeeding audiences
accepted the author's inventions unreser-
vedly and enjoyed them to the full. And,
of course, the victory was not so much one
of Art as of Charm—that indefinable quality
which is one of the most precious gifts of
God to a literary or any other artist. It is
not only faith that can move mountains.
Charm can do so. It can take the reader
or the spectator by the hand and lead him,
credulous and happy, through all sorts of
impossible countries and incredible adventures. More, it can beget in him a genuine
personal affection for the artist which acts

* When *The Professor's Love-Story* was revived at the St.
James's Theatre in the winter of 1903, Mr. William Archer,
himself a Scotsman, called it in *The World*, " a calculated
disloyalty to Art . . . a patchwork of extravagant farce,
mawkish sentiment, and irrelevant anecdote."

like a spell. All the world's outstanding artists, literary and other, have possessed this magical gift. In our own and Barrie's day George du Maurier possessed it in a remarkable degree, and his work both as draughtsman and author was charged with it to the full. After his death Sir Edward Poynter, the President of the Royal Academy, referred to him at the Academy banquet as " the universally gifted and universally beloved." Charm was the crowning one of his many gifts and the main source of the affection he inspired far and wide. It carried his readers, all joyous believers, through the thousand incredibilities of " Peter Ibbetson." Precisely in the same way Barrie's charm led countless men and women prosperously through those of *The Professor's Love-Story* and has led them through many more since then.

The love affair of Professor Goodwillie and Lucy White was not the only sentimental interest in the play. The Professor had a middle-aged spinster sister whose nature had been hardened by a disappointment in love years before, and throughout the earlier scenes of the comedy she was Lucy's

jealous and determined enemy. Then, in
an old forgotten letter-box in the trunk of
the trysting tree, was found a letter which
her lover had left there for her years before,
and which squirrels had buried under their
hoardings, containing the " offer " she had
expected. With that discovery, bringing
its flood of sorrow and joy, the spinster re-
newed her youthful tenderness and promptly
became Lucy's staunchest ally. It is difficult
to conceive an episode more calculated to
stir the Ibsenites of that day to transports of
rage, and Mr. Archer actively disliked it
and said so both now and on subsequent
occasions. Yet the melancholy fact remains that this very episode had probably
as much to do with the success of the play
as any other of its varied ingredients.
Your true playgoer takes with him to the
theatre that sort of faith which is a rich
capacity for believing in what he knows
to be fundamentally impossible and untrue,
and nothing in *The Professor's Love-Story*,
not even the humours of the canny Pete
and Henders, did so much to send its
audiences away satisfied as this particular
little bath of sentimentalism. And so will
it be to the end of Time, whatever the

" botanists " in Wordsworth's poem may
say.

The original Professor Goodwillie was
Mr. E. S. Willard, a gentleman who at one
time promised to be a very important
actor indeed. As the king in " Hamlet "
at the Princess's, as the villain, " The
Spider," in " The Lights o' London," at
the same house, and in the leading parts
in Mr. Henry Arthur Jones's plays, " The
Middleman," and " Judah," at the Shaftesbury, he had given interesting performances.
He had a magnificent voice, and his delivery
of the wronged potter's curse in " The
Middleman " was one of the finest pieces
of elocution I ever heard. Instead, however,
of becoming an important actor he remained
only a very popular one. He was able to
retire early, and people who knew him well
averred that the stage did not interest him
much. I sat next to him once at a little
supper party at Covent Garden Opera-house
and discovered, to my regret, that he was
willing to talk about anything but the
theatre. When one thought of the interesting things he might have said concerning
the theatrical tendencies of the time, and
the many famous authors and players with

whom he had been associated, one had the
sense of wasted hours in hearing him energetically discussing racing ! He evidently
disliked " talking shop." Most of the rest
of the company on that occasion, however,
were connected with the Opera, and they
most interestingly " talked shop " from
beginning to end. At one time the conversation was a bewildering blend of Mas-
senet's " Manon " and the Grand National.

CHAPTER IV.

BABBIE AND HER MINISTER.

IN his next play the dramatist achieved a more solid service to the British Theatre. The production of *The Little Minister* at the Haymarket on the evening of Saturday, November 6th, 1897, proved to be something far more important than a brilliantly successful *première*. It broke down finally the barriers which had so long and so disastrously stood between Literature and the Drama. Mrs. W. K. Clifford was soon to be well known as the writer

not only of many notable novels, but also
of several fine plays, including " The Like-
ness of the Night," in which Mrs. Kendal
at the St. James's was to find one of the
most thrilling parts she ever played and to
give one of her most unforgettable performances ; and Mr. Oscar Wilde already
had a novel and several short stories to his
name as well as his witty comedies. But in
1897 all the leading playwrights of the day
were known almost entirely as dramatists.
Barrie, on the other hand, in spite of his
successes in the theatre, was still chiefly
eminent as a novelist, and the charming
book on which this play was based was at
that very time in its fiftieth thousand.

In the new comedy he attempted the
feat of dramatising one of his own books.
Had he failed he would, as they say, have
put the hours of the English dramatic clock
a long way back. Luckily for the British
drama he succeeded. From that memorable
night dates the brilliant chapter of stage
history in which the names of Clemence
Dane, John Galsworthy, Arnold Bennett,
W. Somerset Maugham, Morley Roberts,
Thomas Cobb, and other men and women
of Letters, so happily shine. It had become

a *cliché* of criticism that no novelist could
make a dramatist.   That night at the Haymarket killed it for ever.   Indeed, when
one thinks of what the first Lord Lytton
achieved in his day, one can only wonder
that such a theory could ever have been
advanced.   The production also excited
keen interest in France.   Writing to
M. Albert Carré in April, 1891, Guy de Mau-
passant had said, "I believe the work
of dramatising the novel is a dead art."   If
only he had been spared to live in good
health until the November of 1897 he would
have had to retract that opinion.

We all know that many novelists have
tried in vain to express themselves effectively in the technique of the stage.   Henry
James was one of these.   His play, "Guy
Domville," produced at the St. James's in
the January of 1895, contained a most
beautiful first Act—beautiful alike in dialogue, characterisation, "atmosphere," and
construction ; but in the second Act his
technique wavered, and afterwards it col-
lapsed, and the play, on the whole, was a
failure ; and of his later contributions to
the theatre only the short play "The
Saloon," produced at the Little Theatre

in January, 1911, did anything like justice
to his immense and exquisite art as a
writer.   Robert Louis Stevenson had also
essayed the Drama with even less popular
acceptance.   That Barrie should dramatize
a novel, and that one of his own, was therefore declared on all sides in advance to be a
courageous and even desperate enterprise.
Most   dramatizations   of   distinguished
popular novels have been complete artistic
fiascos.   Nearly all that is best in the novel
has necessarily to be omitted from the play—
the analysis of character and motive, the
passages of description, the intrusion of the
novelist's own partialities, antipathies and
temperament.   We   have   all   seen   what
dramatists have made of the novels and
characters of Dickens and Thackeray.   Many
of us have also seen what has been done with
two novels of our day, " Trilby " and
" Peter Ibbetson," on the stage.   I will
venture to say that the author of the novel
" The Little Minister " never tackled a
harder or a more self-torturing task than
when he sat down to convert it into a three-
Act comedy.

He succeeded by bravely altering his
story and its characterization to meet the

requirements of an art-form in which everything depends on dialogue and " situation." He had already proved that he was a born dramatist as well as a born novelist, and, with a swoop of instinctive perception, he gathered from his book all the elements of Drama, and left everything else—" purple patches " and all—severely alone. He composed a delicious and genuinely romantic love-story between the young Minister, the Rev. Gavin Dishart, and the pretty " Egyptian," who was to turn out in the end no less a person than Lord Rentoul's roguish daughter, Lady Babbie ; and as a background to this story he depicted the puritanism of the village of Thrums " eighty years ago," and added a picturesque conflict between a community of distressed and desperate weavers and British soldiery representing the Law. Finally he sprinkled the play with humorous touches of Scots peasant character similar to those which had proved so engaging in *The Professor's Love-Story*. The result of it all was that the play took the public by storm, not in London only but in America where it was simultaneously acted in New York, with Miss Maude Adams in the part of Lady

Babbie, and had a run of three hundred consecutive performances. A paragraphist in the *Pall Mall Gazette*, a fortnight after the *première* at the Haymarket wrote, "At this moment the playgoers of London and New York are together paying a sum of £4,000 a week to see *The Little Minister.*" In both cities, and particularly in London, a public still rather haunted by Ibsenism were thankful to take refuge in the sentiment and romance of the play and the purity and sweet atmosphere of it.

For two months before the production the author had been attending the rehearsals from 10 a.m. to 6 p.m. and there was not a touch in the performance which he had not supervised. One thing he had not succeeded in doing. He had failed to convey to his principal performers the intricacies of a genuine Scots accent. His Lady Babbie talked Scots now and then and followed it up with unmitigated English ; his Little Minister had decided before the curtain rose not to attempt Scots at all.*   But what

---

* The Rev. Hugh Shearer, M.A., a Scotsman and a Presbyterian, lecturing on Barrie on February 8th, 1922, in Brighton, said : "When *The Little Minister* was dramatized the critics were surprised that the Minister did not speak Scotch. Of course he did not. In his official capacity every Scottish Minister speaks English."

cared the audience for that? The Babbie of Miss Winifred Emery, tripping barefooted and bare-legged among the reddened leaves of Caddan Woods, in her dress of leaf-green serge, loose bodice, leather belt, scarlet berries in her flying brown hair, and love in her eyes and in her voice, was not dependent upon an accent for her charm, any more than was the trim, black-coated shy young Minister (played by Mr. Cyril Maude) upon whose sense of the proprieties she made such joyous and prosperous war. Those who wanted the northern tang found plenty of it in old Nannie, the cottager, and young Rob Dow, the weaver, and above all in the four Elders of the Kirk, whose names alone are a perfect epitome of their grimly humorous personalities: Thomas Whamond, Snecky Hobart, Silva Tosh, and Andrew Mealmaker. This quartette, in their black suits and stove-pipe hats, and with their unctuous Scots drawl, their canniness, their moral scruples, their diverting hypocrisy, and their unamiable sincerity were a continual joy; and to this day one of the most vivid memories of those who saw the play is the vision of the four queer stove-pipe-hatted heads suddenly bobbing up

from the other side of the churchyard wall
in the concluding scene to spy at their
Minister kissing his now acknowledged
bride, the Laird's daughter. They were
canny to the last. All through the play
they had unctuously and nasally declaimed
against the influence of a " wumman "
upon their Minister ; but when they
realized that he was lawfully married, and
to no less a person than the Laird's child,
they saw the advantage there might be in
it for themselves and the Kirk, as well as
for Mr. Dishart, and their moral scruples
comfortably converted themselves into a
sly and complete approbation.

This play was brought out towards the
close of the year of Queen Victoria's
Diamond Jubilee. It had been a year of
splendid events, a year in which the heart
and pride and imagination of the British
race had been stirred to a very remarkable
degree. As one looks back, it seems a happy
circumstance that a dramatic event of
such literary import should also have taken
place during that year. In connection with
it one regret comes back to me as I write.
There was a story afloat at the time that
George Meredith had asked Barrie to

dramatize his novel " Evan Harrington."
It may have been true or it may not ; but
if such a request was ever proffered, I wish
it could have been acceded to.

Meredith and Mr. Alfred Sutro once
worked together and turned *The Egoist*
into a play into which, Mr. Sutro once told
me, Meredith himself put splendid things,
as, for instance, when Harry de Craye,
summarising in a single sentence his desire
of something more than the " friendship "
Clara offered him, was made to exclaim to
her, " Am I to banquet on that wafer ? "
But those who saw his fragment, " The
Sentimentalists "—the production of which
in London is referred to in a later chapter of
this book—may well doubt whether Meredith was the man to dramatize " Evan
Harrington." His method as a novelist
was essentially a discursive one, and in a
play one literally dare not be discursive
save to a very small extent. He could
write wonderful dialogue as the talk in his
novels shows, but had he the dramatist's
art of cutting and correlating it into mutually
dependent and justly measured acts and
scenes ? Had he the courage to alter the
story of " Evan Harrington " as Barrie

altered that of *The Little Minister* for the
footlights ? Those are the questions, and
it was in these respects that the younger
writer would have been of such brilliant
assistance. As I have said, the story may
or may not be true. In the former case,
what a thrilling *première* the novelists
and dramatists of that day missed ! If
Meredith had been a younger man, the only
person to dramatize one of his novels would
have been himself; but at the time of the
production of *The Little Minister* he was
nearing seventy—and no novelist can tackle
and master the so different technique of
the stage at that age.

CHAPTER V.

A Problem Play.

OUR author's next contribution to the theatre was what is, or was, called a "Problem Play," a foolish phrase invented by that excellent dramatist, the late Mr. Sydney Grundy, and tauntingly flung by him and other persons of a somewhat reactionary turn of mind at the "Intellectual Theatre" (or what they ironically described as such). As a matter of obvious fact every authentic tragedy, drama, or comedy is a Problem Play, for, unless some problem or other is put forward and dealt with, the work can be of no moment and no interest. " The School for Scandal " is quite as literally a Problem Play as anything in Ibsen or Hauptmann, Sudermann or Pinero.

At the Garrick Theatre on Thursday evening, September 27th, 1900, the curtain rose for the first time on *The Wedding Guest*. By this time a Barrie First-Night had become a social event, and the audience was what is called " brilliant " with well-known faces everywhere in the reserved seats. All had gathered in the expectation of a dramatic surprise, nor were they disappointed. Indeed, of the many Barrie First-Night audiences the one of that autumn evening in the days of the Boer War was certainly one of the most astonished. For here was their gentle ironist, their optimist, their sentimentalist ladling out scenes as harrowing and remorseless as those of Ibsen himself !

The wedding guest who so inopportunely arrives at the marriage of the artist, Paul Digby, and the innocent Margaret Fairbairn is the young man's Past in the highly uncompromising form of Kate Ommaney, who had been his mistress, and is

now the mother of his child. When she
sees the bride and bridegroom she faints
and staggers away, but the mischief has
been done, for Paul, like Ibsen's Halvard
Solness, happens to have a sickly conscience
—" one of those consciences that are too
delicately built, as it were, that have not
the strength to take a grip of things and
lift and bear what is heavy."* Accordingly,
when Kate has gone, poor Paul can only
blurt out a full confession of his past
obliquity, lay his present happiness in
ruins, and nearly break his young wife's
heart. In the end Kate passes out of the
story, Margaret forgives her husband, and
all is supposed to end happily.

Naturally such a story from such a
writer not only astonished the audience
but lashed many critics into a rage. The
psychology of its chief character seemed to
have been inspired by that of a memorable
play, one of Ibsen's most splendid, " The
Master Builder," which had been denounced
seven years before as " fantastic balderdash,
devoid of the slightest interest " and " a
bewildering farrago of tiresome rubbish."
The *Times* critic lectured the author of

* From "The Master Builder" (Act II.)

The Wedding Guest on his optimism, and
said he needed to be born again and born
different.   Mr. Clement Scott, in the *Daily
Telegraph*, lectured him still more severely
on his cynicism !   The former of these
declared him no dramatist.   " Mr. Barrie's
main idea (we may almost say his one
idea) " continued this writer " is the
immanent goodness of things. . . . He is
for ever showing the perverse chastened,
the refractory tamed, and the goodness of
the good, but unfortunately, ideas which
make for righteousness do not always make
for good plays. . . . The drama lives by
passion and strife, not by goodness ; force,
not goodness, is the breath of its nostrils.
Native virtue, sheer innocence, is a passive
thing and therefore of necessity a dramati-
cally uninteresting thing."   Such remarks,
dashed off on the spur of the moment, show
how dangerous it may be for a critic to
" let himself go," there being, of course,
quite as much " force " in the goodness of
the good as in the evil of the wicked, and
as much " drama " in sheer innocence as
in sophisticated guilt.   And he wound up
as follows : " The more we see of Mr.
Barrie's talent on the stage the more we

sigh for his talent in the novel. . . There he can give us touches of genius—but only there. . . Mr. Barrie has not genuine, spontaneous dramatic faculty." Alas for Mr. Barrie! Alas, too, for the critic! for the time was to come when he was to write the exact opposite to all this concerning this very dramatist. Mr. Clement Scott, on the other hand, sarcastically alluded to him as a writer "endeared to suburban villas," accused him of teaching immorality and ponderously concluded :—

> The warnings of an older and holier morality that will never die—a morality firm and steadfast when the machine-made ethics of even Scottish dramatists are utterly forgotten—tells every searcher of his own heart that there can never be in this world a full expiation for certain sins.

If the belaboured dramatist read next morning these two judgments upon his play he must have spent a hilarious quarter of an hour. To be described on the same day by one expert as an evangelist of goodness, and by another as an ogre of sin, is a rare experience outside the Party-political world.

Then came the critic on the *Pall Mall Gazette*, who found fault with the play, but took a less extreme view than the writers in the two morning "contemporaries." This gentleman failed to see why the husband should have blurted out his past to his young wife on their wedding-day. Surely, he argued, he might have held his peace if only for the sake of his wife's happiness. At the same time, he found a useful lesson enforced by the play, viz., that a father should not be too lazy to teach his daughter facts often connected with young men's lives ; that Mr. Fairbairn *père* should have pointed out to his Margaret that Digby was an artist, and that artists often. . . and so on and so on. He concluded by withholding all sympathy with the young husband and describing him as the criminal architect of his own misfortunes and his wife's griefs.

One critic, Mr. Archer, gave the play a welcome that was discriminating (Mr. Archer never failed to be that) but cordial. He seemed to see the Ibsen influence and to rejoice in it. Indeed, nothing could have been more Ibsenish than the young husband's wild confession, his sense of unworthiness to be the mate of the pure woman who has married him, or the general paralysis of his reasoning faculty by a hang-dog sentiment of culpability out of all proportion to his wrong-doing. The figure of Kate Ommaney, with its tendency to intermittent madness, and her calm proposal that Paul should spend part of the year with her and the remainder with his wife, are also extremely Ibsenish. Little wonder that Mr. Archer hailed the seeming conversion of the young Scots romanticist with joy. " Hitherto," he wrote, " Mr. Barrie has only trifled with the stage. Now we can offer a very sincere welcome to our new dramatist." *Our new dramatist !* Mr. Barrie had evidently anticipated the tip of the *Times*, and got born again !

In spite of the state of excitement into which it lashed the experts, the play was not a great success, and the explanation of this lay, I think, in the fact that it was indifferently acted. How often has it been the experience of the London playgoer to see the original cast of a play so happily chosen that all subsequent changes in it have been changes for the worse ! The original casts of " The Importance of Being

Earnest " and of Mr. Galsworthy's play,
" Loyalties," were instances of this, and
there was to be another in the case of Barrie's
own next play. But *The Wedding Guest*
suffered from an excess of the sort of acting
which so blackens every shade and whitens
every light that the whole of the dramatist's
appeal to the imagination of his audience
evaporates in a sort of orgie of histrionic
obviousness. If our actors and actresses
would but realise that a play loses all its
real force by over-emphasis on the part of
the players, just as a letter loses by too
much underlining or a man's conversation
by superfluous expletives, how different
would be the history of the stage and the
general estimation of the art of the player !

CHAPTER VI.

Bill Crichton Plays the Game.

*T*HE *Admirable Crichton*, a fantasy in four Acts, was produced at the Duke of York's Theatre on the night of Tuesday, November 4th, 1902. Its *début* took place amid surroundings of the most unpropitious character. The first performance began half an hour late (at 8.30 p.m. instead of 8 p.m.) and was not over until a quarter of an hour past midnight. One result of this was that the reviews of it in the following morning's papers contained the crudest evidence of having been " dashed

off " under considerable difficulties. The
irony of the situation, moreover, was that
the production of a play which, beyond
all others, extols and glorifies a man of the
labouring class had been grossly hampered
by a strike of the stage carpenters ! In a
day or two, however, the domestic situation
behind the scenes righted itself, the production got into smooth working-order and
settled down inside respectable hours of
beginning and finishing, and before the week
was out the new play was being discussed
far and wide. If ever a Problem Play was
set before an audience *The Admirable
Crichton* was one. No comedy of our time
has set its beholders thinking so hard. In
England and America, and even in Paris,
it was hailed as one of the most penetrating
dramatic social pamphlets of the day.

There is no need to retell at length the
story of the Earl of Loam, his family and
friends, or of the butler, Crichton, who, on
a desert island in the Pacific, on which they
are shipwrecked, proves himself their leader
and eventually their King, and becomes the
honoured betrothed of his lordship's elder
daughter, until—boom !—the sudden sound
of an English man-of-war's gun off the coast

signifies the rescue of the party and its
return to England. Immediately all the
old Mayfair rules of caste and relationships
of master and man automatically revive;
the kingly cloak of the ex-butler falls from
his shoulders to the floor, and " washing
his hands with invisible soap " (a way
servants have), he stands humbly before
the woman who, a minute or two before,
had stood as humbly before him. In the
last Act they are all back in the West End,
and Crichton is about to retire from the
Earl's service, marry one of the maids, and
become the landlord of a little public-house
in the Harrow Road.*   The curtain falls

*On Saturday, January 31st, 1920, the comedy was
revived at the Royalty Theatre with a new fourth Act, in
which Crichton was presented as still disposed to lord it
over the Loam household, and from which the allusion to
the Harrow Road public-house and the apparent prospect
of Crichton's marriage with Tweeny had been removed.
In this version Crichton was made to express a deal of
dissatisfaction with the inequalities and absurdities of
English life. Further, he was made not only to foresee the
great war, but to prophesy that when it came all the Bill
Crichtons would get their chance. As he put it : " With
the rolling of the drums England will awaken." These
important alterations in the last Act were felt by several
leading critics to have considerably weakened the play
both as a drama and as an ironical treatise. At the end
of the first performance a letter from Sir J. M. Barrie was
read to the audience in which he hinted at the possibility
of his writing a sequel to the comedy.

finally upon his lordship and his family posing once more as lords and mistresses of mankind, thanks to no abilities of their own, but solely to a social system which appears to elevate caste above character.

The play is full of fine moments. One of these occurs in the love scene of the third Act between Crichton and Lady Mary in the hut on the island. The proud young daughter of a Peer of the Realm has encouraged her father's former butler to think of her simply as Polly Lasenby, and to listen to the voice of Nature. Here is his reply :—

> Polly, some people hold that the soul but leaves one tenement for another, and so lives on through all the ages. I have occasionally thought of late that, in some past existence, I may have been a king. It has all come to me so naturally—not as if I had had to work it out, but as if—I remembered—
>
> > " Or ever the knightly years were gone
> > With the old world to the grave,
> > I was a King in Babylon
> > And you were a Christian slave !" *
>
> It may have been. You hear me ; it may have been.

* The first verse of "To W. A." by W. E. **Henley** (" Poems " fifth edition 1901).

LADY MARY (*who is as one fascinated*) : It may have been.

CRICHTON : I am lord over all. They are but hewers of wood and drawers of water for me. These shores are mine. Why should I hesitate ? I have no longer any doubt. I do believe I am doing the right thing. Dear Polly, I have grown to love you ; are you afraid to mate with me ? (*She rocks her arms, no words will come from her.*)

"I was a King in Babylon
And you were a Christian slave."

LADY MARY (*bewitched*) : You are the most wonderful man I have ever known, and I am not afraid.

Then—boom !—the sound of Fate reverberating from over the waters—the sudden crash that has such tremendous meanings—that makes Earl Loam a Peer again, his daughter once more a young lady of title and rank, and the man who had been a King in Babylon again a deferential menial. As the echoes of the gun roll through the room Lady Mary rushes to his arms. She realizes all that it means, and does not wish to be parted from him. So does he realize it—but he puts her gently from him. " Bill Crichton will play the game," he says slowly ; and his cloak falls from him, his hands rise to the old deferential, servile pose, and his head bows low and lower as the curtain falls. It was indeed a wonderfully fine thing, that third Act, and most beautifully was it played by the late Mr. H. B. Irving and Miss Irene Vanbrugh.

It is of interest to add that when, on June 1st, 1920, a French version of the play made by M. Alfred Athis, was produced at the Théâtre Antoine in Paris by M. Gemier, who also enacted the part of the butler, the quotation from Henley's poem was omitted. On the other hand, when the play was turned into a kinema comedy in 1921, not only was the quotation included, but the film contained elaborate pictures of Crichton and Lady Mary in their early Babylonian relationship of king and slave !

No thinking man or woman could sit through such a play sincerely acted without being momentarily stirred to the depths. Is so highly civilised and organised a society as that of England really a mere fantastic illusion, a house of cards liable to collapse utterly the moment the test of Reality and the touch of Nature are applied to it ? Such was the question which thousands may well have asked themselves as the curtain fell upon that daring third Act

and that bitter fourth, with its allusion to
the little public-house in the Harrow Road.
Mr. Archer solemnly expressed his doubts
of whether the dramatist had the smallest
idea of the immensity of his attack upon
the constituted social order of the country ;
while another critic frankly compared the
play with those writings of Rousseau which
preceded and helped to prepare the way for
the French Revolution ! Surely all such
talking and writing (and there was a great
deal of it) was taking the comedy rather more
seriously than was necessary. After all,
a play based upon such a creature of pure
farce as the Earl of Loam should scarcely
be taken as a serious attack upon the social
order. Had his lordship been presented
as a serious figure, a leading hereditary
legislator, or even an influential personage
in society, the case would admittedly have
been very different, but at the end even of
the first Act poor Lord Loam is virtually an
idiot, and even in the third, and under the
bracing influence of the New Life, he is
little better than a child. He is, of course,
always enormously amusing, but the
"Patriots" did not help to unseat the French
aristocracy by delineating its amusing types.

In fine, the more one thinks over *The Admirable Crichton* the more one enjoys it as a comedy and the less one is perturbed by it as a pamphlet.

It can be enjoyed in the study almost as much as in the theatre. The version of it printed among the author's " Plays " makes a perfectly delightful compromise between the necessarily bare and technical " acting edition " and the highly elaborate volumes, with prefaces bigger than the plays themselves, in which the dramatic works of Mr. Bernard Shaw appear in print. Each character is introduced so graphically that we can see it thoroughly the moment it appears. In some cases we even meet and know it before it comes into view in the play. Here for instance, is the first glimpse we get in the printed book of the epigrammatist, the Hon. Ernest Woolley, the part of which Mr. Gerald Du Maurier was the original interpreter.

A moment before the curtain rises the Hon. Ernest Woolley drives up to the door of Loam House, in Mayfair. There is a happy smile on his pleasant, insignificant face, and this presumably means that he is thinking of himself. He is too busy over nothing, this man about town, to be always thinking of himself, but on the other hand he almost never thinks of any other person. Probably Ernest's great moment is when he wakes up of a morning and realises that he really is Ernest, for we must all wish to be that which is our ideal. We can conceive him springing out of bed lightheartedly and waiting for his man to do the rest.

In another printed version of the play, beautifully illustrated by Mr. Hugh Thomson, the author omitted the reference to the Harrow Road which so saddened many kind-hearted people. Here the scene in the last Act of Crichton's retirement from his lordship's service is set down as follows :—

> CRICHTON : As soon as your lordship is suited I wish to leave service. (*They are all immensely relieved, except poor Tweeny.*)
>
> TREHERNE (*the only curious one*) : What will you do, Crichton ?
>
> CRICHTON (*shrugs his shoulders. God knows! it may mean*) : Shall I withdraw, my lord ? (*He withdraws without a tremor, Tweeny accompanying him.*)

One wonders whether in regard to this Harrow Road reference the author was worried by outside criticism or by doubts of his own. My own opinion—which I only venture to state as that of a very warm

admirer of the play—is that he would have
done better by leaving it alone. We may
be sure that when he wrote it into the play
he did so sincerely and in the impassioned
grip of his theme. Altered play-endings
are seldom improvements. Mr. Bernard
Shaw's example in this matter has been an
admirable one to all writers. No eminent
dramatist has written so many play-endings
which have bewildered or enraged even the
faithful, but the more his critics would
" rave, recite and madden round the land "
the more obstinately he has refused to alter
a syllable. " What I have written I have
written " has been his law, and it is a sound
one.

The original actor of the character of Lord
Loam was Mr. Henry Kemble, a descendant
of John Philip Kemble and his more famous
sister, whose death in 1907 deprived the
stage not only of the bearer of a great name
in theatrical history but of an actor of high
endowments. Mr. Kemble had a rare gift
for extracting the humour of a part and con-
tributing " character," and personality to
it ; and when, as was the case in that of
Lord Loam, the author gave him something
really good to work upon, he could provide

a feast of amusement rich indeed. His face in repose was severe, and his proper personality one of almost archiepiscopal dignity. So completely, however, had he mastered the art of facial, vocal, and gesticulatory comic expression that, however dull or inept the piece in which he appeared, the mere announcement of his name in the cast drew lovers of laughter; and seldom did they go away disappointed. I last saw him on the night of the revival of Mr. Henry Arthur Jones's comedy, " The Liars," at the Criterion, in 1907, in the character of the peevish Archie Coke, who is " discovered " when the curtain rises on the first Act, and I noticed with surprise on that occasion that the audience received him in silence, reserving their welcome for Charles Wyndham. Before the first Act was over, however, Mr. Kemble's drollery was causing roars of laughter, and his share in the final ovation was as warm as that of his brilliant chief. No one who saw him in *The Admirable Crichton* will forget his performance or have the smallest hope of ever again seeing his part so consummately acted. Other skilled performers have essayed it since his death, but the memory of him abides—welcoming his servants in the first Act and losing his mind in his speech to them; crawling through the pampas grass in the second; denouncing the " liars of authors " who had written that two pieces of wood rubbed together produced a light; congratulating himself in the third on the " tit-bits " which his daughter's impending marriage to Crichton would secure for him, and oscillating in the fourth between the airy joviality of the South-sea islander and the windy dignity of a restored Peer of the Realm. The word " great " is sadly overworked and often grossly misapplied to achievements of histrionic art, but the Lord Loam of Mr. Henry Kemble was a great display of comic acting.

CHAPTER VII.

Phœbe of the Ringlets.

THE first performance of the comedy in four Acts, *Quality Street*, took place at the Vaudeville Theatre on the evening of Wednesday, September 17th, 1902, with Miss Ellaline Terriss as Phœbe, Mr. Seymour Hicks as Valentine Brown, and Miss Marion Terry as Susan; and Mr. Archer at once wrote of it, " The play is sure to become a stage classic." It has been revived, as they say, more than once. In November, 1913, for instance, it had another good run at the Duke of York's Theatre, with Miss Nina Boucicault in the part of Susan, Miss Kathleen Nesbitt as Phœbe, and Mr. Godfrey Tearle as the dashing Valentine Brown. In August, 1921, it was brilliantly revived at the Haymarket Theatre, with Miss Fay Compton in the part of Phœbe, Miss Mary Jerrold as Susan, and Mr. Leon Quartermaine as Brown, and was played right through the ensuing autumn and winter and well into the middle of 1922, to a succession of as crowded houses as this popular theatre has ever known.

This last-mentioned revival of the play came at what is called a psychological moment. The long years of the great war, with their records of heroism and endurance at home and abroad, were still vividly in the public memory, and the dramatist's picture of the very similar experiences of our forefathers during and after the struggle with Napoleon had all the thrill of a modern document with the added grace of by-gone manners. During the year 1921, moreover, so many indifferent plays were presented to the London public that the chance of seeing one that contained real feeling and humour and was quite beautifully acted was naturally appreciated. Seen in the light of the actual experience of war, *Quality Street* impressed the Londoners of 1921-2 as a far more realistic thing than it had seemed on that night of laughter and cheers in the little Vaudeville twenty years before. This latter revival submitted the play to the most searching of tests, and it came through it splendidly.

The work is indeed an invention, " a thing which nobody but Mr. Barrie would have written." It bears the stamp of his personality and genius in every scene. Several critics called it an echo of Jane Austen's " Persuasion," but the two stories are almost as little alike as Thrums is like Bath. The similarity between *Quality Street* and any of Miss Austen's works is little more than an accident of period and atmosphere. What appears at first to be its main idea—that a woman found by her lover to have aged and faded may put on fresh youth and reconquer him—is not particularly original. Indeed, as the play proceeds we perceive that such is not its main idea at all. The audience are merely led for a time to believe that it is ; but before the third Act is over they discover to their delight that the author has a very different device in store.

Those who have seen the play will remember that in the first Act demure and pretty " Phœbe of the ringlets " is in love with Valentine Brown and is expecting him to visit and propose to her, but that when at last he appears it is only to inform her that he has joined the Army and is off to the war. In the second Act he returns after nine years' absence, and is visibly shocked to find her almost middle-aged in her aspect and manner. When he is gone, however, she desperately shakes out her ringlets, puts on a pretty frock, and goes to a ball pretending to be her imaginary niece, " Livvy," and there we find her in the third Act, fascinating and flirting with everybody, and above all apparently " setting her cap" at Captain Brown. The crowning beauty of the play is the scene in this Act between the two, in which Brown, believing her really to be " Livvy," solemnly and tenderly warns her against frivolity, and lets her know that it is not she who has fascinated him but the quiet, brave little Aunt she has left at home, the " Phœbe of the ringlets," whose sufferings and fortitude through the long

"SIR, THE DICTATES OF MY HEART ENJOIN ME TO
ACCEPT YOUR TOO FLATTERING OFFER."

years of war have now completely won his heart. The sight of Livvy listening to this declaration with joy and terror—joy because, after all she is not Livvy at all but Phœbe, the beloved—and terror lest, when he knows all, her lover will never forgive her masquerade at the ball—is the dramatic crown of the play. The audience are completely taken in by all that has gone immediately before. The triumph of the heartless Livvy, and the total defeat not only of poor Phœbe but of Captain Brown himself had seemed to be complete. Then, in a twinkling the whole story takes a twist. The entirely unexpected, the perfectly delightful thing happens, and almost before the audience have had time to recover their breath, down comes the curtain. This third Act is certainly one of the most daringly conceived and brilliantly executed things in English Comedy. Mr. Archer even went so far as to declare that there is not a pleasanter and more dramatic turning of the tables to be found in the whole of the English theatre.

Those who saw Miss Fay Compton in this scene will not soon forget her acting. Every tone, glance and movement was significant, and the character in all its complexity lived before the spectator. All through the play Miss Compton acted very quietly. Even in the scene, in the second Act, of the girl's outburst of rebellion at Fate, she was still the eminently genteel, superabundantly " brought up," early 19th-century Scots maiden of the middle class. Her droll cry in this Act, " I should love to inspire frenzy in the breast of the male !" raised a smile rather than a laugh, so quietly was it spoken. (I have heard an actress declaim it, and by so doing draw down a roar of laughter to her own gratification but to the ruin of the character she was impersonating). No actress who has not a sense of the comicality as well as of the tears of life will ever be able to play the part of Phœbe Throssel correctly. Even in her merriest moments she is not a character for an audience to guffaw over. From many spectators she has, when rightly enacted, drawn more tears than laughter, though a good many of these tears have been shed over the last Act and have been tears of happiness.

Similarly Mr. Quartermaine in this delightful revival exhibited this rare quality of understanding. In the second Act, where the returned soldier with the empty sleeve meets Phœbe again and finds her a jaded schoolmistress with her ringlets hidden beneath her cap and all her former pretty brightness gone, he is deeply moved, particularly when she addresses him admiringly as " The brave Captain Brown." In the published version of the play the author has here inserted one of his subtle and characteristic stage-directions. On hearing these words, we read, Brown " *suddenly becomes more of a man.*" His ensuing exclamation shows how he has been touched. " The brave Captain Brown ! Good God, ma'am, how much more brave are the ladies who keep a school !" These are deeply-felt words, and Mr. Quartermaine uttered them in a tone and with a look of absolute sincerity. To those who have previously been watching the anxieties, terrors, and weariness of poor Phœbe and her sister in connection with their pupils (and their pupils' parents) they have the ring of truth.

The character of the elder sister, Miss Susan Throssel, is charged with the tenderest pathos throughout. The scene in the first Act in which she draws from its long hiding-place the wedding-gown she had made for herself years before, but was never to wear,

and offers it to Phœbe as her wedding gift,
becomes from the lips of such an actress
as Miss Marion Terry or Miss Mary Jerrold
one of the most touching.   Here is part of
it, and the reader will notice how much the
dramatist leaves to be made clear by the
art and imagination of the actress.

> Phœbe, I have a wedding gift for you. . . .
> It has been ready for a long time.   I began it
> when you were not ten years old and I was a
> young woman.   I meant it for myself, Phœbe.
> I had hoped that he—his name was William—
> but I think I must have been too unattractive,
> my love. . . . I always associate it with a
> sprigged poplin I was wearing that summer,
> with a breath of a coloured silk in it . . . being
> a naval officer ; but something happened,
> a Miss Cicely Pemberton, and they are quite
> big boys now.   So long ago.   Phœbe—he was
> very tall, with brown hair—it was most foolish
> of me, but I was always so fond of sewing—
> with long straight legs and such a pleasant
> expression.   It was a wedding gown, my dear.
> Even plain women, Phœbe, we can't help it,
> when we are young we have romantic ideas,
> just as if we were pretty.   And so the wedding-
> gown was never used.   Long before it was
> finished I knew he would not offer, but I
> finished it and then put it away. . . . You
> will wear it, my love, won't you ?   And the
> tears it was sewn with long ago will all turn into
> smiles on my Phœbe's wedding day.

The whole of this speech is superficially more notable as an instance of a dramatist's technique than as a piece of literature, yet its purely literary effect on the stage is complete. Such a page gives a valuable glimpse into the method of a modern master of the dramatist's art. It also answers the claim often made by literary critics that a printed play should have a perfect literary form. Such a collocation of words as

> So long ago, Phœbe—he was very tall, with brown hair—it was most foolish of me, but I was always so fond of sewing—with long straight legs and such a pleasant expression.

is certainly not literature in the ordinary sense of the term. It is language written to be spoken upon a stage, and to be illustrated and enriched with the pauses, glances and inflections of a highly-practised actress. Read as people ordinarily read prose, it would excite laughter. Spoken by Miss Marion Terry at the Vaudeville, and Miss Mary Jerrold at the Haymarket, it drew tears.

It is, of course, nonsensical to say (as we have often heard actors say) that the worse a play reads the better it acts. Most of the best modern work for the European stage reads quite as effectively as it acts. Pinero's " Iris," for example, is as touching in the study as it was upon the stage, and Barrie's short plays, *Rosalind* and *The Twelve - Pound Look* make perfect " novelettes." The only difference in this respect between some of the most thrilling speeches in Barrie and those of his contemporaries, is that he reposes more trust in his interpreter than the ordinary dramatist.   His confidence has had a reward rich indeed.

CHAPTER VIII.

An Uncomfortable Play.

MR. BERNARD SHAW has classified certain of his plays as "unpleasant." Similarly the author of *Little Mary* announced it beforehand as "uncomfortable." That, like the play itself, was one of his jokes. The audience at the first performance at Wyndham's Theatre on September 24th, 1903, found it the very reverse of uncomfortable. They followed its Prologue and two Acts with the liveliest amusement and received its final revelation with one of the loudest and longest peals of laughter ever heard in a theatre. The piece, it is true, was followed by an aftermath which was " uncomfortable " enough. For at least a year no comic song in a music hall was complete without one or more references to somebody's " little Mary " and a good many mournful pleasantries of the dinner table were similarly traceable-back. But the play itself was of the merriest, and any man who went to see it expecting something *à la* Ibsen (or Shaw in his " unpleasant " vein) must have received one of the æsthetic shocks of his life.

In the Prologue we meet Moira Looney managing a *crèche* at the back of the shop of her Irish grandfather, a chemist and a man of genius. Moira's speech betrays her nationality, but she never tells anyone she is Irish, for she holds it " sinful to brag." Her Grandpa is passionately fond of the dear Saxons, and has written, for their benefit, a " pamphlet " in three large folio volumes, entitled, " The Medium—or How to Cure our Best People," and in the first Act of the

comedy we find Moira applying the princi-
ples of this pamphlet to a number of aristo-
cratic *malades imaginaires*, and claiming
to be working with an invisible Medium
whom she calls Little Mary. In the second
Act we find that she has cured all her
patients. The *ci-devant* languid and self-
indulgent ones now breakfast at eight, dine
in the middle of the day, and have become
brisk, useful and happy persons. How has
it all been done? asks Lord Carlton. "By
Little Mary" is the answer, and Lady
Milly murmurs ecstatically "To me, Little
Mary is a religion!" "But how, when so
many specialists failed, has a quack
succeeded?" persists Lord Carlton with an
eye fixed critically on Miss Looney. Then
that young lady lets out her secret. Grandpa had a deep conviction that the dear
darling English people—and particularly
the nobility—suffered from eating too much.
He foresaw an awful fate impending for
England if ever the working-classes, as a
result of over-eating, should become as
stupid as the Best People. Grandpa's great
maxim, his golden rule, was not One Man
One Vote, but One Day One Dinner. He
called it "Home Rule for the English."

In short, Little Mary was the stomach ! Take care of that, treat it with wisdom and moderation, and all will be well ! Such was the climax of this artfully built up little comedy.

There were many persons present at the first performance who said as they left the theatre that as soon as the joke was out— and, of course, every daily paper in London would publish it on the morrow morning— future performances would necessarily fall flat. However, nothing of the kind happened, and for months crowded audiences received the *dénouement* with laughter almost as boisterous as that of the first night. They knew perfectly what was coming and enjoyed it all the more when it came. There is, of course, nothing exceptional in this. For years the same phenomenon has been observed in the case of the Savoy Operas, of which the jokes are known word for word by at least half the audience, and roared over when they come as though they were being heard for the first time. It is the old story of honest Diggory and Mr. Hardcastle's anecdote of Ould Grouse in the Gunroom, " I can't help laughing at that—ha ! ha ! ha ! for the soul of me.

We have laughed at that these twenty years—ha ! ha ! ha !" After all there is a good deal of honest Diggory in most of us, and a good joke in a play or a book can be laughed at not for twenty years merely, but for a life-time. Obviously, too, there is the contagion of laughter in a crowded theatre to help the joke along.

In one respect the dramatic humorist is in a more difficult position than that of Mr. Hardcastle. He has to tell his funny story through the lips of his actors and actresses, and we all know how a third party can make or mar the best of jests. Happily the original cast of *Little Mary* was as near perfection as it is possible to be. Two impersonations particularly stand out in one's memory—the Moira Looney of Miss Nina Boucicault and the Sir Jennings Pyke, a fashionable medical specialist, of Mr. Eric Lewis. Miss Boucicault's diction of crystalline clarity enabled every word she said to be heard in every part of the house ; her voice, with its musical Irish inflexions, was a continual delight, and her expressive face completed the illusion.

I hope that the shade of Charles Lamb

revisits London whenever such acting as that of the late Mr. Henry Kemble or Mr. Eric Lewis is to be seen in a worthy part and a worthy play. How unerringly he would have perceived and how delightfully he would have commemorated the comic airs and graces of this latter most accomplished comedian ! In *Little Mary*, and a year or two later as Sir Bloomfield Bonington in Mr. Shaw's " The Doctor's Dilemma," Mr. Eric Lewis gave revelations of art and personality which one could enjoy again and again. Such performances, in which every glance and tone and movement has its significance and contributes its touch of character, are the best answer to those who rate the actor's craft not merely as the meanest of the arts but as so little of an art as scarcely to be one at all. To watch Mr. Eric Lewis as a fashionable physician pretending to decline a proffered fee, as a *nouveau riche* windily rebuking snobbery, or as a foolish but self-confident gentleman urging another to clear his mind of cant, is to see at work a comic art sufficiently expressive and varied to have delighted even Elia.

The last delicacy of acting, in which the

sudden lighting or dying-out of a smile, a quick half-turn of the head, or the unexpected raising of a hand or lowering of a tone may imply a whole volume of meaning, is the more delightful for its rarity. The American comedians, Mrs. G. H. Gilbert and Mr. James Lewis, who used to visit London in the " 'eighties " and " 'nineties " of the last century with Mr. Augustin Daly's company, had the secret of it. Theirs was a nutty ripeness. Mr. Eric Lewis's processes are more sophisticated. They could and did act in classic Comedy as well as in modern Farce. Mr. Eric Lewis, would, I think, look odd in anything but the latest fashionable attire and sound exceedingly odd in blank verse. But the three names stand for a technique as distinct as that belonging to any other branch of art and as worthy of admiration.

Even as I write the names occur to me of two other players who have exhibited a similar exquisiteness (there is really no other word for it) of comic art—Miss Lottie Venne and Mr. Rudge Harding. Those who saw Miss Venne as Mrs. Parker Jennings in " Jack Straw " at the Vaudeville, and Mr. Harding as the ineffable Pringle

in " The Brass Bottle " in the years before
the war, know what I mean by an art which
seems to get the maximum of effect by the
minimum of effort—though the qualified
spectator knows how vast a quantity of
thought, experiment and native humour
lie at the back of it all the time.

CHAPTER IX.

The Never-Never Land.

THE most familiar of our author's writings for the stage, the fantasy *Peter Pan, or the Boy who Wouldn't Grow Up*, was produced at the Duke of York's Theatre on Tuesday, December 27th, 1904. It captivated its first audience, and has put thousands of other audiences in England and across the seas under a similar enchantment. In London it has been revived each succeeding winter as a Christmas entertainment, and despite inevitable changes in the

cast in the course of so many years, a peculiarly affectionate relationship has existed
from the first between the public and the
players. *Peter Pan* is nearly as well known in
New York and all the great cities of America
as in London. It has had more than one
successful season in Paris. There is a statue
of its youthful hero in Kensington Gardens ;
the " literature " of the play is inter-
national, and in every respect the piece
may be regarded as a classic of its kind.

Anything more dreary than the sort of
entertainment from which this fascinating
play helped to rescue the children and
grown-ups of London can scarcely be im-
agined. The typical Christmas pantomime
was a version of some fine and famous
story, mangled almost past recognition,
spattered with the banalities and vulgarities
of the Lion Comique of the music-halls,
set in a blaze that half blinded and to music
that half deafened the spectator, and generally lasting from four to five hours and
sending everybody home more or less a
wreck. In the place of these inflictions,
Peter Pan offered the nursery of Mr. and
Mrs. Darling's three children, Wendy, John
and Michael, where the nurse, or Nanna,

was a Newfoundland dog that turned the hot-water taps on and off, laid out the children's night clothes to warm before the fire, and saw that they took their medicine at the proper time. Through the open window comes flying the motherless Peter Pan and the fairy Tinkerbell, and away with them fly the three children to the Never-Never Land, with its Pirates and Redskins, fire-eyed wolves, smiling crocodile with the clock ticking inside it, the cottage for Wendy with a hat for its smoking chimney, the jolly parlour and dormitory for her and her family under the roots of the pine-trees, and last, but not least, the deck of the pirate schooner, with the terrifying Captain Hook offering his fearsome handshake, and the pathetic and affable Irish pirate, Smee, smiling through his benevolent spectacles and tearing his pieces of linen over the sewing-machine.

The Redskins proved to be far more amiable than they sounded; the wolves ran away from anyone who stooped and looked back at them from between his legs, and the fiercest of the Pirates promised in agitated tones to live henceforth a blameless life if only Wendy would be a mother to him ! Nor were music and dancing lacking, the piece being sprinkled with jolly tunes by Mr. John Crook, jovial dances for the Pirates, the Red Indians, and the children, and rollicking songs, of which the Pirates' roaring chorus beginning " Avast ! Belay ! Yeo-ho ! Heave-to " is the best of all. And who that ever saw the piece will forget Peter's frantic appeal to the audience to save the life of the dying Tinkerbell by proclaiming that they believe in Fairies and expressing their faith by clapping their hands ? With what a promptness and passion we, young and old alike, used to declare our belief and clap with all our might ! And what a rapturous further round of applause there used to be when the tinkling and twinkling of the reviving " Tink " proved that our demonstration had achieved its object !

From time to time the author added new features. In the first revival for example, at Christmas, 1905, the scene of the Marooner's Rock or The Mermaid's Lagoon was added, with the famous exclamation of Peter, as he stands on the rock with starvation staring him in the face, "*To die will be an awfully big adventure !*" Another addition

was the beautiful final scene of the Tree-
tops, with Wendy and Peter in their house
amid the leaves, and a thousand little lights,
each a fairy, tinkling as the curtain fell amid
a carillon as of countless silver bells. To
pass from that scene to the murk of St.
Martin's Lane on a muggy winter night did
indeed seem, even to the prosiest, like leaving Fairyland behind.

Fantasy as it is, *Peter Pan* has inspired
some rare acting. Miss Nina Boucicault's
performance as the hero was a triumph of
temperament, insight, and art, and that of
Miss Maude Adams* in America was, by all
accounts, equally remarkable. The Wendy
of Miss Hilda Trevelyan was another joy
of the original production in London ; Miss
Pauline Chase was a later popular Peter ;
while up to the time of the writing of these
lines, London has happily known no Smee
but that of Mr. George Shelton, the original
Tesman of our author's first dramatic venture in 1891, and the gladsome Ben in his

*Mr. H. Massac Buist, writing in the *Pall Mall Gazette*
of December 2nd, 1913, said : " I have seen America's
first and only Peter Pan, Miss Maude Adams. She can
convey the notion of impishness and suggest a creature
partly human and partly elfish in a manner which no other
actress except Miss Boucicault is able to do."

second in the year following. The original
Captain Hook was Mr. Gerald du Maurier,
and his performance was also much admired,
Mr. Archer describing it (and very justly) as
" a highly finished intellectual achievement." He was succeeded in the part by
the late Mr. Robb Harwood, who played it
in several revivals and elaborated his performance into one of the richest pieces of
burlesque seen in London in our time. Mr.
Harwood's impersonation had weird imaginative moments that lifted it altogether
above the ordinary. He was a tall man with
a fine presence, and never shall I forget his
aspect as he stood suddenly transfixed with
terror, on the deck of the schooner at the
sound of the cock crowing in the cabin, or
the awe-inspiring tones in which he cried—
staring upward with only the whites of his
eyes visible—" Will no one bring me out
that Doodle-doo ?"

When the piece was first presented at the
Vaudeville Theatre in Paris on Tuesday,
June 16th, 1908, as " L'histoire d'un petit
garçon qui ne voulait pas grandir," Mr.
Harwood was the Hook, and the French
critics were enthusiastic over his performance. One writer admirably described it

as a " Cruikshank caricature come to life,"
while another paid it the great compliment
of saying that it had set him thinking of
Frédéric Lemaître.   The first Paris production had a five weeks' season and was
revived in the following June to the delight,
of course, of the large English and American
colonies in the city.   The story of the play
has also been translated into French and is
a popular children's book in France.   In it
Hook becomes Lecroq, Smee's name is
spelt Smie, and the " Doodle-doo " of the
original dwindles into a very unoriginal
" coq de malheur."   Where Hook cried,
" Will no one bring me out that Doodle-
doo ?"   Lecroq merely remarks, " Il faut
que quelqu'un m'apporte ce coq de malheur."   However, " Doodle-doo " is not an
easy expression to translate.   The French
coquerico is not half so funny.

Some London critics found fault with the
sight of the empty cots as the curtain rose
on the Darlings' nursery in the last Act
as too poignant in such a play, and one
wrote : " There will be few audiences in
which some eyes will not fill with tears of
remembrance in this scene."   One must
feel every respect for such a criticism.   The

author, however, had the joyous return of the children in store, and when that moment comes, its intensity is, of course, all the greater for whatever suspense may have preceded it. He was, we think, justified in considering only the effective development of his situation. As a whole, I think *Peter Pan* is not only one of the prettiest, but one of the happiest, of Tales for Children, and its tendernesses no less than its drolleries only enhance that final impression.

Reference has been made to the Peter Pan statue in Kensington Gardens. It is the work of Sir George Frampton, R.A., and stands at the south-west end of the Long Water. The hero of the play is depicted as a sturdy little fellow, blowing a horn (surely one of Tennyson's " horns of elf-land "), and on his symbolical pedestal rabbits frisk, mice frolic, doves make love, a fairy confers with a squirrel, and children peep forth from just such a hole in the earth as Wendy's living-room under the pines. This work of art, so lovingly and learnedly wrought, was presented by the dramatist as a gift to the nation, and was set in its place on the eve of May Day, 1912. The occasion was marked by no public

A HORN OF ELF-LAND.

unveiling or ceremony of any sort. To people who had known its site, the monument seemed next day to have arisen magically in the night. Children passing there the day before had seen nothing save the bushes and the trees, the grass, the water, and the ducks ; and lo ! on this May Day, their friend, Peter Pan was there, with his tunic flying in the air, and all his queer fascinating associates, four-footed and winged, frolicking below !

Thousands of people, young and old, visit this monument and many of them ask each other what it all means, for neither the subject nor the sculptor is named. The only readable intimations in its immediate neighbourhood are " Visitors are not allowed to walk on the Grass " and " Dogs are not allowed unless with a Lead." Not a quarter of a mile away stands G. F. Watts's great group of the horse and his rider, which he called " Physical Energy," and the visitor observes that the title of the work and the name of the sculptor are attached for all to see. However, Sir George Frampton's gay little figure does not appear to mind. He just goes on blowing his fairy horn to the creatures round his pedestal, the big and little human beings on the path in front of him, and the ducks that quack for crumbs all day on the edge of the shining lake.

CHAPTER X.

Miss Ellen Terry Sits by the Fire.

IN the October of 1905, Henry Irving, the chief of the late Victorian actors, died at Bradford and was buried in Westminster Abbey. With the passing of that romantic and commanding personality the artistic level of the London stage dropped perceptibly. The theatre of a country can only be at its highest while a supreme tragic actor or actress is revivifying for it the noblest works in its dramatic repertory, its great tragedies. Such was the theatre of Rome and Naples under Ristori and Salvini, of Paris under Rachel, of New York under Edwin Booth, and of London under Irving.

While, however, on the classic side our stage suffered this heavy loss, the year was a fairly notable one on the modern. Among the new plays produced during its twelve months were " Man and Superman," " Major Barbara," " The Walls of Jericho," and " The Voysey Inheritance," and on Wednesday evening, April 5th, at the Duke of York's Theatre, was given for the first time Barrie's comedy in three Acts, *Alice Sit-by-the-Fire, or A Page from a Daughter's Diary*, with Henry Irving's enchanting comrade in Art, Miss Ellen Terry, in the part of Alice Grey, the middle-aged but still charming lady who had just returned from India with her husband, Colonel Grey, to their children in London.

Once more a new Barrie play was to be greeted with a highly polyphonic chorus. One critic hailed it as its author's most joyous composition, another called it his saddest, a third delighted in its artlessness, and a fourth praised it as an elaborate *reductio ad absurdum* of the methods of

M. Sardou ! In other words our àuthor was still insisting on ganging his ain gait. Even W. S. Gilbert and Bernard Shaw were easier to classify than this wayward Scot who so insisted on being a law unto himself, setting at defiance every recognised rule and prescription of dramatic craftsmanship, playing all sorts of practical jokes upon his audience, and at the same time manipulating the stops of laughter and tears with so unrivalled a mastery.

Alice Sit-by-the-Fire indeed proved one of the most bewildering of his plays. It opened as a comic fantasy, developed into a highly complicated and artificial entanglement, and ended as a very pretty and rather pathetic comedy. The second Act is a masterpiece of old devices and new effects. Its basis is comic, yet its development would be Tragedy if it were not Farce, and often the audience can scarcely declare which it is ! In this brilliant *tour de force*, Amy, the seventeen-year-old daughter of the Colonel and Alice, a young lady whose ideas of real life are taken entirely from plays (she has lately seen five, all at " thinking theatres," in one week) goes (in evening dress of course : that is always worn on these painful occasions) to the rooms of a bachelor, a Mr. Stephen Rollo, to "save" her beautiful but misguided mother, and get back her "letters" (there are always "letters" in these cases) from "the scoundrel." Needless to say, the mother is as innocent as the daughter, while "the scoundrel" is the most innocent and harmless of the three.

Upon this comic foundation rises an endless series of misunderstandings, each wilder yet seeming more plausible than the last. Amy nearly drives Stephen out of his mind by her accusations, until footsteps are heard on the stairs and she rushes to hide in a cupboard, leaving one of her gloves on the floor. The new arrival is her father, the Colonel, who has dropped in for a chat with his friend, and presently catches sight of the glove, recognizes it as a lady's but not as his daughter's, and proceeds to rally his host on being a man of gallantry. Then Alice also drops in, accidentally discovers her daughter in the cupboard, immediately imagines the worst, and sets to work to "save" her poor misguided child ! This she seeks to do by suddenly whisking the girl into the room as somebody who

has "just come." Presently, however,
Amy picks up her glove and begins to put it
on, and her father, seeing this, realises that
his child has been in Stephen's rooms prior
to his own arrival. Is Stephen a villain?
"No," cries Amy, still intent only on
"saving" her mother. "No! He is my
betrothed!" Hereupon Alice believes more
firmly than ever that her daughter has
"gone astray." Amy still entertains the
same belief in regard to her mother, while
Mr. Rollo has gathered from Amy that her
mother is wildly in love with him!

These are but a few of the emotional
issues in this tangle of a footstep on the
stairs, a dropped glove, and a cupboard.
Seldom has been seen such a piling-up of
situation on situation. Certainly since the
scène à faire between the manicurist and
the nobleman in "The Gay Lord Quex"
London had seen nothing at once so artificial
and so consummate. The scene of Amy's
nonchalant drawing-on of the glove and all
that followed was a piece of technique after
Sardou's own heart, and thrilled its
audience, just as the finding of Lady Windermere's fan in Wilde's first play, and of
Major Maurewarde's letters in the later

Pinero, " His House in Order," thrilled
theirs. After this excitement came the
charming last Act, with all the little misunderstandings of the previous scenes swept
away, and the middle-aged Alice, sitting
by the fire, realising that her day as a Queen
of Hearts is over, and that henceforth her
rôle is not in the ball-room or the conser-
vatory but by the fireside. As she says, half
to her husband and half to herself :—

> It's summer done, autumn begun, farewell
> summer ; we don't know you any more. My
> girl and I are like the little figures in the
> weather-house ; when Amy comes out Alice
> goes in. Alice Sit-by-the-Fire henceforth. The
> moon is full to-night, Robert, but it isn't
> looking for me any more. Taxis farewell !
> Advance four-wheelers ! I had a beautiful
> husband once, black as a raven was his hair.
> Pretty Robert, farewell ! Farewell, Alice that
> was ! It's all over, my dear. I always had a
> weakness for you, but now you must really go.
> Make way there for the old lady !

To hear that speech, with its laughter and
tears, delivered by Miss Terry and, as it
were, set to the music of her smiles, and
tossings of the head, and pretty characteristic gestures, was to enjoy as delicate a
treat as the stage of that day had to offer.

If *Alice Sit-by-the-Fire* did nothing else it proved its author's exceptional versatility. From what other dramatist has there come a succession of plays so various as those we have so far been considering? Burlesque, farce, comedy, comic opera, romance, ethical pamphlet, sociological treatise, fantasy for children, and technical drama *à la* Sardou—and nearly all of them brilliantly successful! It is really an extraordinary record, unapproached by any other British dramatist. It is, of course, part of the quality of " unexpectedness " in him which is part of his charm, and which emerges, not only in his treatment, but in the choice of his subject.

The play did well in America, where Miss Ethel Barrymore played the part of Alice, but in spite of the acting, not only of Miss Terry as the mother, but of Mr. Aubrey Smith as the Colonel and Miss Irene Vanbrugh as the daughter, it was not a great success in this country. There is a curious story told concerning it! It is said that when the dramatist had completed the writing of *Peter Pan* for Mr. Charles Frohman, he took it to him at the Garrick Club, together with the manuscript of *Alice*

Sit-by-the-Fire as a gift, with the profits of which the manager could recoup himself the losses he was certain to incur on *Peter Pan* ! The story may be true or it may not. What is beyond dispute is that *Alice Sit-by-the-Fire* only ran for a short season and that *Peter Pan* made more than one fortune and was to run for years !

CHAPTER XI.

The Man who could not Laugh.

IN *The Admirable Crichton* the protagonist was a man. In the comedy, *What Every Woman Knows*, produced at the Duke of York's Theatre on the evening of September 3rd, 1908, she is a woman. John Shand has his points, but it is his wife, his Maggie Sit-by-the-Fire, who, as the Greeks used to say, gets her foot into the right position and sets the earth swinging.

The heroine of this comedy in four Acts is one Maggie Wylie, a demure Scots lassie with old-fashioned curls, a passion for poetry and romance, and twenty-seven birthdays. Her father and her brother would be thankful to see her married and settled, but, as they sorrowfully admit, she has " no charm," and wooers are not forthcoming. One night, however, a young man by name John Shand, a railway porter during the summer and a student at Glasgow University in the winter, comes stealthily in through the Wylies' parlour window, not to " burgle " but to enjoy a few hours' clandestine study of the books in their excellent library. The men of the family, catching him in the act, and knowing him as one of their neighbours and a smart young fellow, compel him to take a seat and give them his attention while they make him an offer. They are prepared to hand him over £300 so that he may complete his University course comfortably, on the con- dition that he consents to marry their Maggie at the end of five years should she wish him to.

Up to this point the outstanding person of will, character, and ideas has been young Shand, while the demure, homely little Maggie, sitting by the fire knitting a sock,

has seemed a person of very small importance, and by no means one of those " sweet
little simpletons who have their fingers in
the destiny of a man."* The observant
spectator, however, has noticed that every
word the young lady says is to the point,
every action significant, even each glance
charged with meaning. There are visible
possibilities in this little fireside Maggie. . .
So ends the first Act, the best in the play,
and one which bears the hall-mark of its
author on every page.

In the second, John is already an M.A.,
is elected an M.P., and Maggie duly becomes
Mrs. Shand. He, poor fellow, imagines he
has carved out his political career and been
the architect of his success, and no one so
confirms him in this delusion as his wife,
though anyone with half an eye can see
that she has been doing it all, giving him
his ideas (which are the gold of his speeches)
and doing it all so tactfully that he
regards himself as an inspired creature and
her as his inferior. And when, in the third,
he becomes infatuated with the beautiful
Lady Sybil Lasenby (apparently a member
of the Loam family), the artful little wife

*Ibsen's " Hedda Gabler." (Act III.)

plays her master-stroke. She persuades her friend, the Comtesse de la Brière, to invite the " lovers " to her country cottage for a fortnight, and, sure enough, at the end of the two weeks, John has not only discovered that Lady Sybil bores him to death, but has been told by an eminent member of his Party that a speech he has prepared and proposes delivering at a great meeting at Leeds, is curiously lacking in his customary originality and force.   The latter disclosure is a frightful shock, and when Maggie reappears he gets another.   For he is made to realise that it is she who has helped him up the ladder and placed him where he is.   She does not tell him so.   On the contrary she goes on flattering him.   " If only I could make you laugh," says Maggie, " our life together would be so much rosier."   But it is part of John's pride that he has never laughed in his life.   " I never was one for fun.   I have not a spark of humour in me," he says ; and one muses with a sigh upon the many shrewd little pleasantries his witty Maggie must have wasted upon him since the night she captivated the men who had just returned him to Parliament with a speech of two words, " *My constituents !* "

However, just as the curtain is preparing to come down, she makes one more effort— offers him a feeble little joke, such as one would regale a child with : " I believe the first woman was made, not out of one of Adam's ribs, but out of his funny-bone !" And at *that*, John Shand, M.A., M.P., the hope of his Party and one of the hopes of his country, condescends to smile, then to laugh, and finally to fling his arms aloft in a howl of enjoyment ! Ah, Maggie has him now ! He does not know it, but her triumph is complete. And as the curtain finally falls he is in her arms.

There are lines in this play which one remembers years after. David Wylie's remark to young Shand in the first Act : " A young Scotsman of your ability let loose upon the world with three hundred pounds, what could he not do ? It's almost appalling to think of. Especially if he went among the English." Another gem is the slow soliloquy with which James Wylie brings the curtain down on this Act :—

> It's a most romantical affair. . . . I wonder how some clever writer has never noticed how queer women are. . . . It's my belief you could write a whole book about them. . . . It

was very noble of her to tell him she's twenty-six (*muttering as he wanders away*).   Yet . . . I thought she was twenty-seven.

And how audiences have laughed at David's remark to the Comtesse in the second Act, " My lady, there are few more impressive sights in the world than a Scotsman on the make."

The part of Maggie was acted with rare humour and sense of character by Miss Hilda Trevelyan who, in the absence of the author, received the chief ovation at the end of an exciting first night ; and Mr. du Maurier made another of his Barrie hits in the character of John Shand.   The story is told in Mr. Marcosson's life of Charles Frohman that Barrie was so delighted by Miss Trevelyan's performance on the opening night that as soon as the curtain had fallen he cabled his enthusiasm to Frohman in New York, and that next morning the young actress found a cable from the manager on her breakfast table, doubling her salary.

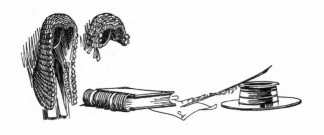

CHAPTER XII.

A Gilbertian Jest.

THE experience of September 4th, 1913, remains one of the most curious in the memory of Barrie first-nighters. At the Duke of York's Theatre that evening were produced two short plays *The Will* (with which I deal in another chapter) which was completely successful, and the three-Act comedy, *The Adored One*, which, though acted by a company which included Mrs. Patrick Campbell and Sir John Hare, was almost as complete a failure. For the first time, the final fall of the curtain on a Barrie play evoked nearly as much hissing as cheering, and the audience came away bewildered and depressed.

The story will show that on this occasion the author allowed the " freakishness," which is one of the most attractive of his qualities, to carry him too far. A lady of magnetic charm, whom every one calls Leonora, was travelling in a train with a little daughter who was suffering from a cold; and a gentleman sitting opposite to her refused to let the window be closed. The mother insisted; he remained obdurate; and at last she opened the door, pushed him out and killed him, re-closed the door, drew up the window, and calmly continued her journey. At the inquest she gloried in her deed; and in the dock of the Old Bailey, charged with murder, she sat smiling across her bouquet at her friends, quoting Horace to the judge, and obstinately answering the prosecuting counsel's charge with the cry, " But my little girl had a cold !" In the end she was triumphantly acquitted.

This court scene, which occupied the second and third Acts, was Gilbertian burlesque. When the accused took her place in the dock the whole assembly reverently rose; the counsel for the Defence offered her his hand in marriage as she stood in the witness-box; the judge ogled her as his Lordship in "Trial by Jury" ogles the plaintiff, and the jury begged for her to be allowed to sit with them while they considered their verdict. Could all this be considered amusing as the sequel to an act of murder?*

Perhaps an actress with a less "intense" personality than that of Mrs. Patrick Campbell might have carried it off with a gaiety, though one doubts even that. The jokes at the expense of the Law with which these two Acts were sprinkled added to their gloom. There was a scene in which the judge questioned a witness who happened to be a solicitor and was known as "Honest John." "Is that to distinguish you from

---

*After the first night the author set to work immediately and re-wrote the play, and three weeks later a revised edition of it was brought out and certainly made a far more diverting entertainment. In this, Leonora's story of the murder was shown, after all, to be only a joke; the trial was presented as the dream of a disturbed sleeper, and after it came an entirely new Act in which Leonora's most ardent worshipper arrived at a happy agreement with the lady. This new version was a remarkable example of rapid re-writing, but, as usual, it failed to turn the play into a success. The word had gone forth that *The Adored One* was not one of its author's happier efforts, and it soon disappeared from the London bill.

other members of your profession?" asked
his lordship. When the same witness remarked that he had played a game of golf
with the deceased, the judge asked: " Did
you carry smashers and putties in your bag?"
and again: " Did you play a fearsome? I
have always understood that when four men
play golf together it is called a fearsome."

Such pleasantries as these coming from
any playwright would have been sufficiently
depressing. Coming from the author of
The Admirable Crichton they were like

> . . . the fatal wound
> Which spread dismay around.

Just before the end of the play, we had an
elaborate speech from the judge, in which
he addressed the acquitted and beaming
heroine as a sort of abstraction—a figure of
myth. " You are not the woman of
to-day," said his lordship in the most
solemn tones of Sir John Hare. " She is
something wiser and better. When *she*
speaks we hear the voices of a thousand
nightingales. *You* are already a legend,
and we bid you Hail and Farewell!" All
of which (and this is only a scrap from a
prolonged flood of eloquence) sounded
like sentimentality gone wrong. For, after

all, women have not voices like nightingales,
nor do they care to be told that they have.
Neither do they care to be told that they are
exceptionally wise, or abnormally good, any
more than they would care to be even
jocularly charged with murdering a man
for preferring fresh air in a railway carriage.
I came away from the theatre that evening with that distinguished barrister, judge,
editor and playgoer, the late Sir Douglas
Straight, and I can still hear the tone with
which he remarked, " A melancholy evening ! A very melancholy evening !"*

What did it all mean ? The author had
as we have seen been sitting at the feet of
Woman, contemplating reverentially her
moral, intellectual and spiritual superiori-
ties over the mere male. In other words
the Feminist wave had caught him in its
clasp and temporarily washed away his

The Adored One was subsequently further revised by
the author, and produced in New York under the title
of *The Legend of Leonora*, with Miss Maude Adams in
the character of Leonora. The character of Leonora
also reappeared in the short play, *Seven Women*, produced at the New Theatre on April 7th, 1917, in
which the same woman had seven separate personalities, rather recalling the passage describing the three
Thomases and the three Johns in " The Autocrat of the
Breakfast-Table."

sense of humour. After all, there is very little, if any, superiority in a good woman over a good man. Their respective virtues are equal in quality. There is nothing of purity, courage, steadfastness, kindness and all we sum up in the word honour in which the two sexes do not equally excel. The deep devotion which most men feel for their mothers does not uphold the Feminist view, as many women have a similar special tenderness for their fathers. Even women who have been tyrannically treated by their fathers—Elizabeth Barrett Browning and Clara Schumann, for example—have revered and loved them, and longed and striven passionately for a reconciliation, even while adoring the husbands from whom their fathers would have torn them asunder.

CHAPTER XIII.

ENTER MDLLE. GABY DESLYS.

THE fact is, I fear, we have struck a
barren patch in the garden of our
author's planting. We shall soon be out
of it and among the flowers again; but
it must be admitted that there was very
little fragrance or colour in *The Adored One*,
and that in the revue that followed it there
was less still. Happily, the gardener was
soon to be himself again, but for a time his
benevolent genius was certainly in abey-
ance.

Never shall I forget the first performance
of *Rosy Rapture, or The Pride of the Beauty*

Chorus. It took place at the Duke of York's Theatre on Monday night, March 22nd, 1915, and the title-part in the piece was enacted by Mlle. Gaby Deslys, a young French artiste of the variety theatres, whose fame had been gained largely by costumes which allowed the exposure of a liberal expanse of back, and hats which transcended all other feminine headgear in vastness, complexity, and brilliancy of colouring. I had seen her perform without discovering that she could act, heard her warble without realising that she could sing, and seen her dance without detecting in her the skill, or grace of any one of a dozen other known dancers of that day. The *Times* critic once wrote of her :—

> "No doubt for special tastes Miss Deslys offers special provocations. The devotees of dress must worship her. Amateurs of bare-backs must find her priceless. English people who like to have their language tortured out of recognition must revel in her."

And to find such a person the centre and star of a revue by the author of *Quality Street* was indeed among the oddest of experiences One can only say that the great war was upon us, and the world was already beginning to turn upside down.*

The most successful feature of the piece itself was an American kinema picture of an adventurous chapter in the life of a baby. Some scenes burlesquing the version of " David Copperfield " then being acted at His Majesty's, with old Peggotty for ever driving Little Emily out of his home so that he may keep up his heartrending search for her, and lighting his pathetic signal-candle in the window while she is actually seated in the room watching his agonies, also had their humours. But of all the impressions of the evening, one only remains vividly in my memory, and it had nothing to do with either the revue or its performance, though it had much to do with Mlle. Deslys. The curtain had fallen on the final scene, and the usual

---

Rosy Rapture was destined to be the last of the many Barrie plays to be produced by Mr. Charles Frohman. He was returning from America to England on the " Lusitania " when, on May 7th, 1915, the great Cunard liner was torpedoed by a German, and sent to the bottom of the sea eight miles off the Head of Kinsale. Mr. Frohman was one of the hundreds of men, women and children sent to their deaths in this huge act of criminality. His last recorded words were the brave quotation from *Peter Pan :* " To die will be an awfully big adventure ! "

applause had caused it to be raised again to reveal the smiling heroine of the evening bowing and " blowing kisses." Having duly absorbed this vision a number of people in the stalls turned to make for home, only to find their passage up the staircase barred by a procession of men bearing huge trophies of costly flowers for the star of the evening. These were solemnly, and not without difficulty, handed across the orchestra, until the stage literally looked like a flower-show, with Mlle. Deslys in the middle of it, bowing and smiling more energetically than ever. At last the procession ended, the last trophy was conveyed over the foot-lights, the staircase was declared " clear," the curtain fell to rise no more, and we were able to escape.

CHAPTER XIV.

CINDERELLA'S BALL.

THE great war had reached its middle period when our author's next play, the fanciful *A Kiss for Cinderella*, was produced at Wyndham's Theatre on Thursday evening, March 3rd, 1916. In it we find him unmistakably himself again. This is not the place in which to dwell upon the strenuous way in which Sir J. M. Barrie threw himself into the cause of his country and the Allies during those years, doing much work on both sides of the Atlantic; but it can be said here that this play, and the one which immediately succeeded it, were, in their way, contributions to Victory, for they helped to keep the nation cheerful and even sweet of heart amid the horrors of those times.

In the spring of 1916 a large proportion of the young manhood tarrying in or passing through London were either on leave from the Front or destined soon to be on their way to it. Meanwhile the great city had settled down to the nocturnal darkness which was maintained to the end of the war, and which made the lighting-up of the ordinary street and shop lamps on Armistice night seem the gayest and most joyous illumination London had ever known.

> Above the roofs of Lincoln's Inn
>   From cloud to cloud the searchlights flare,
> While far below, with silvery din,
>   The chimes of Dunstan call to prayer.
> O sights of war and sounds of peace !
> When shall your dreary discords cease ?

In those nights of 1916 a respectable middle-aged citizen was in danger of being arrested for striking a match (assuming he was so lucky as to possess one !) in the street for the purpose of lighting his pipe ; but, by way of compensation he could also stand in

the middle of Piccadilly Circus, and, looking
skyward, see Orion and the rest of the
spangled firmament as clearly as from a
hill-top on the South Downs. London
itself at that time took on a new grandeur
in the moonlight. To see the classic façade
of the British Museum, the pillars and dome
of St. Paul's, or the towers and pinnacles of
the Abbey and Palace of Westminster under
such conditions was to realise anew the
beauty of those buildings. Of course it
was grateful and comforting to have the dear
old familiar glare of Shaftesbury Avenue
and the Strand restored, but, as usual, there
had been compensations for its absence.

The audience that groped its way to
Wyndham's Theatre that March night
found the war as evident in the play as in
the streets. This new Cinderella was a
poor waif known to her neighbours as
" Miss Thing, the Penny Friend " because
she kept a *crêche* in which the charge *per*
baby was a penny a day, and also mended
" dickies " and shaved people for the same
charge. The small inmates of her *crêche*
were all " babies of the Allies "—all, that is
to say, save one, a small Gretchen, of whom
we were told, rather nervously, " She is

Swiss—at least—not *exactly* Swiss, but—
well, *you* know. While the other babies
are cooing and smiling and " talking beautiful French'" this poor ill-conditioned
Gretchen is for ever " strafing " people.
A kindly policeman looks in (he is after a
" spy "), gives this unfortunate mite a
friendly pat, and—she bites him ! In fact
she has to be kept under a " wire entanglement." But be not alarmed ! The " wire "
is only worsted !

Cinderella of course falls in love with the
policeman and presently drops asleep and
dreams she is at the Prince's Ball, and there
in the next Act we meet her again. The
ball is the queerest any Cinderella ever
attended. It is just such a vision as a poor
waif of mean streets might imagine. The
ballroom is lit by street lamps, shaded as in
war-time, but with gold instead of black
paint. The King and Queen look precisely
like the royal pair on a pack of cards, and
their thrones resemble seats in a Tube
railway-train and have straps suspended
from overhead with which their Majesties
steady themselves while standing. The
rival princesses wear large prize-cards like
the prize animals at a horse-show, and when

at last the Prince appears who should he
turn out to be but the kind policeman,
beautiful in green silk breeches and a bob
wig ! And she dances the fox-trot with him
and then wakes from her dream. We
next meet her in a seaside sanatorium re-
covering from pneumonia caught by sleeping
(and dreaming) in the snow ; and here the
policeman visits her, " proposes," and is
accepted. And being like all members of
the Force, a Romantic, he gives her a pair of
glass slippers instead of the usual common-
place every-day engagement ring, and behold, they are very happy, and down comes
the curtain.

Of course it was a war play, but it was
one which even the soldiers could honestly
enjoy. How they roared over the patriotic
English baby in the *crêche* singing " Ye
Mariners of England " until the patriotic
French baby could endure it no longer and
struck up " The Marseillaise " with amazing
energy ! How all the comic kindliness of
the Penny Friend and the broad drolleries
of the Prince's ball—the vision of a poor
illiterate cockney imagination with its sug-
gestions of playing-cards and Tubes, street-
lamps and straphangers, and a young

policeman as the Prince—how they all
appealed to the men in khaki who, night
after night, half filled the house !

More than one writer compared Miss
Thing's dream with the vision of the dying
child in Gerhart Hauptmann's famous
dream-poem called "Hannele," but the
two plays are so different, not in detail
merely but in spirit, that the comparison
falls to pieces. The German play is a
tragedy charged with the bitterest irony—
a veiled but bitter attack upon society and
religion. *A Kiss for Cinderella* is a comedy,
all brotherliness and toleration. Everybody in it is kind (save the biting Gretchen !)
and, in his or her own way, happy. The
Royalties and the Policeman are as agreeable and sympathetic as "The Penny
Friend." Even the jokes at the expense
of the arch-enemy of those years were as
void of malice as those of the average British
Tommy, whose concerts behind the lines
were incomplete without the ferocious bass
or baritone declamation of the notorious
German Hymn of Hate translated into
English, and sung amid peals of irrepressible
laughter.

Of Miss Hilda Trevelyan's numerous

impersonations in Barrie plays, none was prettier or more appealing than her Miss Thing, while Mr. Gerald du Maurier as the romantic policeman was a joy from first to last. The piece went on tour through Great Britain and was as gratefully welcomed in other towns and cities as in the metropolis. The two elements of the theatre which did most to hearten the public during those years were the Gilbert and Sullivan operas and Sir J. M. Barrie's plays. They caused a laughter which involved no loss of self-respect, and kept up a relationship between the idealism of the great mass of the people and that of the theatre at its best. In *A Kiss for Cinderella* thousands of people were taken out of themselves and the cares of the time for three happy hours ; and when they had to get back to the realities of life were able to do so with lighter and braver hearts. The writing of this and of the play that followed was, among other things, an act of real patriotism.

" The best hearts," said Uncle Toby, " are ever the bravest," and a people who can keep their hearts cheerful while they are fighting are generally a mighty uncomfortable enemy to have to face. Barrie's greatest war service was the stimulus he gave to this spirit on both sides of the Atlantic. It was recognised as gratefully in America as in Great Britain.

During the rehearsal of this as of all his plays the author altered his dialogue as new ideas struck him. The contrast between him and Pinero and Shaw in this respect is very marked. Pinero's way has been to present his players (and also the leading critics) with an early printed copy of the whole play. Shaw has often helped himself by having the first rough draft of a new play printed and then working on it in the process of development until he lays down his pen ; the thing is finished, and the rehearsals begin. Sir J. M. Barrie, on the other hand, has more than once been writing a play on odd scraps of paper up to the day of its production—and long after !

CHAPTER XV.

THE MAGIC WOOD.

THE comedy, *Dear Brutus*, produced in the autumn of 1917, takes its title from the lines addressed by Cassius to Brutus in Act I., scene 2, of " Julius Cæsar " :—

> Men at some time are masters of their fates.
> The fault, dear Brutus, is not in our stars,
> But in ourselves.

and the " idea " of the play is one which Lord Dunsany also used in his comedy, " If—," produced some four years later at the Ambassadors Theatre : " If only at a certain moment I had acted differently, or circumstances had been different, how

much more happily everything would have
turned out !" There is, of course, nothing
new in this. It was an old idea when Plato
and Sophocles mildly put it aside more than
two thousand years ago. Yet millions upon
millions of men and women have given
utterance to it with a sigh. At the best
such speculations can be but guesswork.
Only too often the wish is father to the
thought. There is always the fact to be
reckoned with that personality goes on—
that it develops more than it changes.

> Ah! Zeus knows, and Apollo, what is dark to
> mortal eyes ;
>
> They are Gods.

Personality is far more the decisive factor
than any chance of a moment. The hero
of Lord Dunsany's play once missed a
train that was to have enabled him to keep
a certain appointment : years after he
recalled the fact and wondered what his
fate would have been had he caught that
train : then the play showed us his " other
life "—and certainly it was romantic and
highly-coloured enough ! In the end, however, " If—" taught us nothing, for it proved
in the end that all the adventures we had

seen were merely the dream of a sleeper as
he lay stretched upon the sofa in his modest
suburban parlour. And mightily glad was he
to awake and discover that it had only been
a dream !

In *Dear Brutus* this theme is handled a
great deal more thoroughly. We meet a
number of dissatisfied and ill-assorted
people who have been invited down as
guests to the country seat of a Mr. Lob,
a queer little gentleman of middle-aged
aspect who is manifestly, as even his name
suggests, a sort of grown-up Puck.* There
is, for example, a Lady Caroline who has
naturally spurned the love of Mr. Lob's
pilfering butler, Matey. Then there is a
Mr. Purdie, who is always sighing for some
woman other than his wife, and musing how
happy he would have been had he married
differently. There is a Mr. Coade who is
quite contentedly married and ascribes his
tranquillity of mind to that fact. There is
Mr. Dearth, a painter, who has taken to
drink and whose career is ruined, and who
sighs over and over again, " If I only had

*In " A Midsummer Night's Dream " (Act II., sc. 1)
the Fairy, addressing Puck, calls him, " Thou lob of
spirits."

had a child," while Mrs. Dearth, grown into a hard and selfish woman, petulantly reflects how much more happy her life would have been if only she had married the Honourable So-and-So. And after dinner **Mr.** Lob sends them all for a stroll in a Magic Wood at the back of the house. This happens on Midsummer Eve, when we know, on Shakespeare's authority, the " fairies are frolic."

It is in this Magic Wood, at this magic hour of the year, that the vital scenes of the comedy take place. Here Lady Caroline finds herself married to "the Matey that might have been," now a prosperous financier, and worshipping him without being much the happier therefor. Mr. Coade finds himself wifeless but contented, for the secret of happiness is in himself and his own cheerful temperament. Mr. Purdie is married to one of the " other women " and is as miserable with her as he had been with his earth-bride. So we see all these people with their ways of life changed and their lots in no respect the happier. One and one only, Dearth the painter, who had longed for a child, is blessed in the fulfilment of his longing. In the Magic Wood he

meets an enchanting young girl, Margaret
(a name beloved of poets), all charm, and
frolic, and love, and lo ! she is his longed-
for daughter !

The scenes between this pair, the father
and the child, literally " made " the play.
Within a week all London was talking of
them ; within a month one heard of them
in far-off parts of England. Nothing could
have been sweeter than the spirit in which
they were conceived, or more exquisitely
delicate than the art with which they were
composed. And indeed one can accord
praise as high to the way in which they
were acted by Mr. du Maurier and Miss
Faith Celli. The whole episode was a
genuine materialisation of a poet's vision.
In the last Act, too, when all the queer
people were back from the wood, the better
for their adventures in it, there came a delicious touch just before the fall of the
curtain. We saw Dearth and his wife,
happy together once more as they had been
in their early married life, walking away
arm-in-arm to make a new and better start
and—tripping behind them, the radiant
dream-daughter of the Magic Wood. The
cheered playgoer passed from the bright

theatre into the dark streets feeling that the painter's longing was going to be fulfilled for him after all.   Thus, if ever a play had a happy ending *Dear Brutus* had *

Like its predecessor this comedy was produced while the war was still raging.   It was first acted at Wyndham's Theatre on the evening of Wednesday, October 17th, 1917.   London then was still a city of nocturnal darkness.   Russia was crumbling to her ruin, but the British Air Force were bombing Germany, and the United States of America had entered the struggle on the side of the Allies six months before.   The conflict was to last another year, and Death with his scythe had yet a fearful harvest to gather in.   But the vision of the inevitable end was clearer than ever, and the national confidence unwavering.   And once more, thanks to a Barrie play, London heartened itself to face the tragedy of life with a glimpse of its tenderness and beauty.

Dear Brutus was revived at Wyndham's Theatre on Saturday evening, May 6th, 1922, with Mr. du Maurier and Miss Celli in their original parts.

CHAPTER XVI.

The Call of the Island.

EVERY admirer of this writer's work probably has his favourite among the plays. With the majority this is assuredly *Peter Pan*, though there would also be a big poll for *The Admirable Crichton* were the question put to the vote, and possibly one nearly as large for *Mary Rose*. This piece was first acted at the Haymarket on the evening of Thursday, April 22nd, 1920, and on the final fall of the curtain the house rang with such cheers as a London theatre had not heard for six years. Next day the papers contained the customary mingling

of blame and praise. One writer called it
" Barrie at his best," another declared
that the dialogue had a tendency to drag
and the sentiment to cloy. A third con-
fessed he could not understand a scrap of
it, and a fourth called it a powerful pamphlet in support of Spiritualism ! After
that it only needs to be added that the play
ran through the remainder of the year and
well into 1921.

I have heard that the origin of the play
was as follows: The author was sitting one
evening with a lady, who presently said
to him : " Sir James, you have done many
things for the theatre, but there is one that
still awaits you—the writing of a ghost-
story. I wonder if you would try your
hand at that ?" Her listener might have
replied that, in a sense, he had already done
it, as his first acted play had contained a
ghost, but his simple answer was : " I don't
know ; I will have a try "—and the result
was *Mary Rose*. The story may or may not
be true, but the play is certainly a ghost
story, and one of the best and most original
in the modern dramatic repertory. The
most thrilling piece of this class I had seen
on the stage by a contemporary dramatist

was Henry James's one-Act play, "The Saloon," a dramatization of his short story "Owen Wingrave," to which I have already referred in an earlier chapter, and in which the ghost, although it directly brought about the tragic conclusion, was not seen by the audience. In *Mary Rose* the phantom not· only appeared but wept and talked. The Prologue prepared us for its apparition, the three Acts of the play proper gave us its life-story, and in the Epilogue it actually appeared.

The story of the play proper is as queer as that of the Prologue and Epilogue. The mystery of a little island in the Hebrides—

"And we in dreams behold the Hebrides"—

from which visitors who hear its "call" are spirited away no one knows whither, to reappear months or even years after looking not a day older, was obviously not acceptable to all tastes. I have heard more than one very sensible lady dismiss it scornfully as "rubbish." One night, too, during the second Act, while the heroine was rapturously addressing the mossy pillow on which, more than twenty years before, she had sat as a child visiting the island, I distinctly heard somebody in the row

behind me mutter " What an idiot !" Indeed,
it may as well be said here that if the would-
be spectator of a characteristic Barrie play
is not prepared to meet the dramatist half-
way he or she were wiser to remain outside
the theatre. You must accept his pre-
misses if you are to enjoy his developments
and believe in his conclusion.

The scene between the young husband
and wife on the island in the second Act,
is one of the most beautiful things our author
ever wrote. There is hardly a word of
love in it, yet it could only have been spoken
by two people who loved each other completely. The subsequent disappearance of
the wife at the " call " of the island, and
the terror and anguish of the husband,
made a still deeper impression ; while the
scene in the third Act in which the girl's
mother, now an old woman, hears in London
that she has re-appeared in the Hebrides,
is unchanged after five and twenty years,
and is being brought home, is surely one of
the most affecting ones ever written for a
theatre. When the wife was spirited away
on the island she left behind her not only
a young husband but a baby son, and on
her strange return to the three who had

WHERE DREAM-FIGURES HOLD REVEL.

long mourned her as dead, now changed into old parents and a middle-aged husband, she learns that the baby has grown into a man, gone to Australia, and long since been lost touch with. These tidings kill her. In no other play is Sir J. M. Barrie's "almost unendurable pathos" so manifest as in *Mary Rose*.

In the Epilogue another quarter of a century has elapsed and we find her ghost moving in and out of the now long-empty and deserted rooms of her old home, looking for the child. At last she meets him—a young Australian soldier, who, passing through London in the days of the great war, has discovered the old home of his parents, found it reputed as haunted, and sits by an empty grate smoking a cigarette and waiting sceptically for the ghost. The scene that ensues heals the phantom's aching heart, and when, just before the curtain falls, she hears the "call" of the island again, she turns and glides slowly away, not, however, towards the bleak Hebrides and more years of unsatisfied yearnings, but towards a night-sky glittering with promise and beautiful with stars. So the curtain fell upon this beautiful composition, to a note of sadness that melted into one of joy. Many a time it fell amid the complete and unbroken silence of a crowded audience. The play had cast a spell which it needed the familiar chords of " God Save the King " to remove.

Mary Rose held the stage of the Haymarket Theatre for more than a year, and at a time when an unparalleled wave of materialism was influencing the whole national life. The success of such a play at such a time was a proof that even then the Soul of the nation was as alive as ever. It was, of course, beautifully acted. Art more exquisite than that displayed by Miss Mary Jerrold in the part of Mary Rose's mother; a personality more appealing than that of Miss Fay Compton in the character of the bewitched daughter; and studies of character more pleasant or more finished than those given by Mr. Leon Quartermaine, Mr. Arthur Whitby, Mr. Norman Forbes and Miss Jean Cadell were not to be seen on any stage. Naturally, the large section of London playgoers who understand and appreciate good acting crowded to see them, and many, like the present writer, must have gone repeatedly to a play that was as

unique as its playing. Discussion raged
round it in the correspondence columns of
newspapers ; the theories of its meaning
were as numerous as they were strange,
and people wrote impassioned letters to the
author, begging him to " explain himself."
For months the purport of the play was as
lively and as general a theme of controversy
round the dinner tables of London as the
policy of Mr. Lloyd George ; and when the
play toured the United States it left a similar
trail of heated speculation in its wake.
The calmest person amid all the hubbub
was the gentleman who had written it. The
rewards of the successful dramatist are
many, but one of the richest must be his
silent but amiable contemplation of a world
wildly agitated as to what the deuce he is
driving at.

The one undeniable fact, however, is that
thousands came away from it with hearts
full of gratitude to the dramatist—the
original genius who had given them this
exquisite mingling of laughter and tears,
prayer and moonlight, London and the
Hebrides, an Australian " digger " and a
delightful couple of connoisseurs in old
prints, love wounded to the heart, joy

transformed into terror and anguish, and a pale low-voiced ghost sitting happily on a soldier's knee.

A dear amusing friend, now " beyond these voices," used to say that if ever he had to fly from his wife the " cause " would be the statue of Thalia in the vestibule of the British Museum ! Such caprices are part of the imaginative life, and they are only very bereft and unhappy folk who can make a mock at them. In precisely the same way the ghost of *Mary Rose*—the creation of a few words on paper—cast her spell upon thousands.

CHAPTER XVII.

FOUR LITTLE MASTERPIECES.

AS Balzac and Henry James were masters
not only of the *roman* or novel but
also of the *conte* or short story, so Sir J. M.
Barrie has shewn himself a master of the
short play as well as of the long. None of
our leading dramatists has written so many
plays in one Act, or attained to anything
like their uniformity of excellence, both
comic and tragic. Many of these pieces
have been written for a single performance,
generally in aid of some patriotic or philan-
thropic fund. Others have been performed
repeatedly. *The Twelve-Pound Look*, for
example, and *Rosalind* are almost as well
known as the best of his longer works.

In this chapter I will say something of four which I consider to be the best of them —*Old Friends, The Twelve-Pound Look, Rosalind,* and *The Will.* The writer's versatility appears as strikingly in these as in the longer plays, and he excites the terror and anguish of his audience as surely as the laughter.

On Monday, March 1st, 1910, a notable triple bill was submitted at the Duke of York's Theatre, consisting of a dramatic fragment by George Meredith called " The Sentimentalists," preceded by Barrie's one-Act tragedy, *Old Friends,* and succeeded by the same author's one-Act comedy, *The Twelve-Pound Look.* Of the Meredith fragment this is not the place in which to speak. Suffice it to say that while it lacked the touch of the born dramatist, it breathed a literary fragrance that made its beautiful sentences a joy to listen to.

Old Friends, on the other hand, was a concentrated tragedy by a master-craftsman. Its story was that of a daughter's inheritance of the vice of dipsomania from a parent who had, as he declared, shaken off the habit years before. For twelve years the unfortunate father has not touched an intoxicant. The desire for them is dead; the only living souls who share with him the miserable secret of his past are his wife (who had helped him in the fight with his enemy) and his friend, Carroll, a clergyman. But as poor Stephen Brand chats with his friend by the fire in his sitting-room late at night, after his wife and child have gone to bed, he blurts forth a strange thing. Shadows have been about him lately. He has seen them, *heard them*, moving as he has lain in bed awake in the next room. Are they the shadows of dead sins? His friend says No, cheers him as best he can, and at last returns to his rectory. Left alone, Stephen locks the doors, turns out the light and enters his bedroom, then returns to the dark sitting-room and throws himself wearily into a chair by the dying fire. In a few moments a door at the top of a flight of stairs opens stealthily and a white shrouded figure appears, slowly and silently makes its way down, and approaches the little cabinet in which the spirit decanters are kept. The mysterious " shadows " have materialised, and Stephen Brand, starting from his chair, sees his own child furtively trying to get at the cabinet.

A horror beyond words chills him—an agony of remorse. He questions her and she lies to him—just as he had been wont to lie in the years of his own degradation. Then the wife comes down. She has known her daughter's malady, and has had the girl sleeping with her for security's sake. When she realises that her husband also now knows what has happened, she turns on him and reviles him for the " legacy " he has given their child. " But I broke myself of the habit !" cries the wretched father " Never !" is the wife's bitter reply. " Never ! The habit *left you*. It had worn you out. You could entertain it no more, and it left you. Our vices *leave us*—we don't drive them away. Their consequences remain—shadows that speak—old sins that have become Old Friends." It is a ghastly story and was told with tragic power, but was it not needlessly pessimistic and needlessly cruel ? It is surely not a fact that men never drive away their vices—that they merely leave us when they have exhausted us. Many people have fought and overcome this very vice of dipsomania and have become perfectly reliable and useful members of society, and in many

cases none but themselves have known the
anguish which the battle has cost them.
In spite of Mrs. Brand in *Old Friends*, no
man or woman is more worthy of admiration
than one who has fought this terrible fight
to a successful issue.

In *The Twelve-Pound Look* we meet Sir
Harry Sim, an aggressive, self-confident,
genial "bounder," who has been highly
successful in business and has just received
the honour of knighthood. He has been
twice married. His first wife, after a time,
managed to scrape together twelve pounds,
bought a typewriter, and then ran away
from him and let him divorce her. She
had not flown to another man ; the intellectual and spiritual limitations of one member
of the sex had been sufficient for her. Her
successor, once bright and pretty, has
become pale and nervous, and is manifestly
as suffocated and bored in her domestic
life as her predecessor had been ; and
towards the end of the play, after various
nervous preliminary inquiries, she asks her
husband the price of a typewriter. He
unsuspectingly answers, and she drifts
slowly from his presence with a queer look
in her eyes. As she vanishes an idea strikes

him. Then the awful truth breaks upon
him. This one is going to leave him as the
first had done, and he stands gorgonised
from head to foot as the curtain falls. This
little comedy is just a Barrie joke, not
lasting much more than half an hour, but
packed to the brim with wit and irony.
It might of course be objected to it that if
either of Sir Harry's wives had possessed a
scrap of humour she might have rendered
her husband and her life with him more
tolerable. After all, he was not a bad
husband, as husbands go. At any rate
he made a handsome home for his wife,
gave her all she could desire on the material
side, and philandered with no other women.
A wife able to put a little brain into her
love could have made a good deal of such
a partner. All that Sir Harry's victims
could do was to suffer and run away. Apart
from that, however, the play is perfectly
logical, while its wit can be enjoyed again
and again. It has been revived repeatedly.
In the first twelve months of its career
such well-known actresses as Miss Lena
Ashwell, Miss Lillah McCarthy and Miss
Irene Vanbrugh were seen in the character
of the first wife, and Miss Mary Barton gave

a memorable impersonation of the second—
a piece of acting so delicate and wistful that
one remembers it vividly still.

Rosalind was produced at the same theatre
on the evening of October 14th, 1912. Its
story is that of the momentary disillusion-
ment of a young man on discovering that
a bewitching actress with whom he has
" fallen in love " is, in her private life,
a person of more than forty and a dowdy.
We had seen a somewhat similar situation
in *Quality Street*, and much the same plot
in Charles Reade's short play, " Nance
Oldfield," in which Miss Ellen Terry used
to draw down the thunders of the Lyceum
in the Irving days. Barrie, however, went
farther than Reade, for he showed his
actress changing her dowdy attire for
fashionable garments, brilliantly rekindling
the young man's passion, and bringing the
curtain down upon a blissful couple of
lovers. There were many telling lines in
the play, and the study of the actress who
talked like an ordinary human being so
long as she was in her drab dressing gown
and had only her landlady for audience,
but became a queen of romantic airs and
graces the moment she had her male

adorer to pose before, was a brilliant one;
but how it would all have prospered with a
less accomplished player than Miss Irene
Vanbrugh in the title-part, I dare not con-
jecture.   This gifted actress, so rich in
wit and humour and wisdom of her own,
who, when she and the author were almost
equally unknown to playgoers, had acted
so cleverly in his first work for the stage,
the Ibsen burlesque at Toole's, now shed
the whole glow of her heightened personality and perfected art upon his latest
creation, and the result was inspiring in the
extreme.   Miss Helen Haye in the part of
the landlady gave a performance almost as
rich in "character" though, of course, on the
quieter side.   This little play came at the
end of a triple bill which had also included a
ghost play by Sir A. W. Pinero, called
"The Widow of Wasdale Head," and a
wildly amusing farce by Mr. Bernard Shaw,
called "Overruled."   It sent the great
audience away in one of those states of
excitement which are the crown of a rare
first night.

Another of these notable little pieces was
The Will, produced at the Duke of York's
Theatre on the evening of September 4th,

1913. Its three short scenes contained the
material for three long Acts. In the first
a young and devoted husband, accom-
panied by his pretty and fond young wife,
called on his lawyer four months after
marriage to give instructions for the making
of his will. With the exception of a small
bequest or two, all is to go to her, and she
can only weep at the thought that one
day she will be a widow. In the next scene
years have passed and he has called again.
Another will is required ; he has become
rich, she is splendid in furs and their son
is at Harrow. He still desires to leave
her everything, but only as a life-interest.
He fears that if his £70,000 were to pass
to her unconditionally, she might spend it
foolishly, and the thought fills him with a
greedy terror. She, however, talks him
round, and once again they retire. And
the third scene shows him for the last time
in the lawyer's office, a widower, " child-
less " (his son has gone to the dogs, his
daughter has married a chauffeur), friend-
less, and weighed down with the monstrous
burden of his wealth. " Let it all go to the
six men whom I have beaten most cruelly
in life ! And let them have it with my

curse for each of them!" he screams, "for money does not bring happiness!" Here again was a poignant story, told with many a delicate touch, and beautifully acted, especially by Mr. O. B. Clarence as the lawyer and Miss Helen Haye as the wife who hardens so tragically as she grows older.

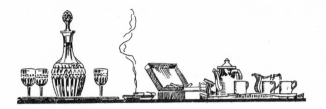

CHAPTER XVIII.

OTHER SHORT PLAYS.

A FANTASY that had a somewhat artificial
pathos at the back of it was the comedi-
etta, *Pantaloon, or A Plea for an Ancient
Family*, originally produced at the Duke of
York's Theatre on April 5th, 1905, as a
curtain-raiser to *Alice Sit-by-the-Fire*, and in
which Mr. Gerald du Maurier played the title-
rôle and Miss Pauline Chase made a graceful
Columbine. In 1921 it was revived at the
Old Vic. and quite as well acted, but there
it followed Shakespeare's "A Comedy of
Errors," and its humours seemed curiously
small after those of the mighty Elizabethan.

Another piece in one Act is *Shall we join the Ladies?* which is said to have been intended as the first Act of a play in four Acts of which the other three remained to be written. It was first acted at the opening of the theatre of the Royal Academy of Dramatic Art in Gower Street on Friday, May 27th, 1921, before an audience that included the Prince of Wales, and for this particular occasion it was given the following cast :—

Sam Smith (the host)	MR. DION BOUCICAULT
Lady Jane Raye	... MISS FAY COMPTON
Mr. Preen	MR. CHARLES HAWTREY
Lady Wrathie ...	MISS SYBIL THORNDIKE
Sir Joseph Wrathie	... MR. CYRIL MAUDE
Mrs. Preen	LADY TREE
Captain Jennings ...	MR. LEON QUARTERMAINE
Mrs. Castro... ...	MISS LILLAH MCCARTHY
Mr. Vaile	MR. NELSON KEYS
Mrs. Bland	... MISS MADGE TITHERADGE
Mr. Gourlay	SIR J. FORBES ROBERTSON
Miss Isit	MISS IRENE VANBRUGH
Miss Vaile	... MISS MARIE LÖHR
An Officer	MR. NORMAN FORBES
Lucy (a maid) ...	MISS HILDA TREVELYAN
Dolphin (a butler)	MR. GERALD DU MAURIER

It was put into the evening bill at the St. Martin's Theatre on March 8th, 1922. Its plot is of the queerest. The scene is a rich dinner-party, and, as at old Werle's in the first Act of Ibsen's " The Wild Duck," thirteen people have sat down. Obviously something dreadful is going to happen. It does. Presently the host informs his guests that a brother of his had been murdered at Monte Carlo two years before, and that one of those present is the murderer or murderess ! The play shows suspicion falling first on one then on another, and as the curtain descends an unexplained and blood-curdling scream is heard from an adjacent room. The piece was hailed as Farce by several critics. It impressed me rather as a study in the grim and grotesque. Smith seemed to me to be out of his mind, and I felt it quite possible that his whole story was a malignant invention intended to frighten a crowd of people who had been sponging on him for his wealth. At the St. Martin's Mr. Leslie Faber gave a memorable piece of acting in the uncanny part of the host.

The little melodrama, *Half an Hour*, was produced at the Hippodrome in September, 1913. In this, as in *The Twelve-Pound Look*, we were shown a suffering wife. Exasperated at last beyond bearing, Lady

Lillian Garson writes a letter to her husband telling him of her flight and giving the name of the man, Hugh Paton, an engineer, to whom she has gone. At Paton's rooms she is rapturously welcomed, and the lovers prepare to leave London at once for Cairo. Paton runs out to call a cab, is knocked down by a motor omnibus and killed, and the doctor who comes back to the rooms with the body, divines the heart-broken woman's secret, but keeps silent. There is nothing left for her but to return home, where she is lucky enough to find that Garson has not yet seen the letter she had left for him. She changes her frock, and rejoins her husband, who has invited some friends to dinner, and when these arrive one of them happens to be the very doctor whom she had met under such terrible and compromising circumstances an hour before. Once more he realises the situation, and once more he keeps silent. His knowledge of the husband convinces him that she is a woman more sinned against than sinning. Presently she is able furtively to recover possession of the self-incriminating letter; and the curtain falls upon the party going in to dinner with boisterous talk and laughter. I have called it a melodrama, for coincidence waved its magic wand a good deal more freely in it than should be the case in genuine comedy or real drama, but it was a striking little piece of its kind, and worthy of the author's gift for inventing effective situations.

The New Word, first acted at the Duke of York's before *Rosy Rapture* in March, 1915, was a touching little picture of an inarticulate abashed father and son bidding each other good-bye before the boy left for the Front. *The Fatal Typist*, produced at a matinée at His Majesty's in November, 1915, in aid of the Australian wounded, was one of the author's practical jokes ; and *Shakespeare's Legacy*, given at Drury Lane in April, 1916, at a matinée in aid of the war work of the Y.W.C.A. was another, but less riotously funny. *A Slice of Life*, given as a surprise to the audience at a matinée at the Duke of York's in June, 1916, proved a most diverting skit on the use of the telephone on the " modern " stage, each character in the play confiding all his or her secrets to the audience by telling them into a telephone receiver.

The Old Lady Shows Her Medals, produced

at the New Theatre in April, 1917, was another of the author's touching plays of the great war, and the acting in it of Miss Jean Cadell as the charwoman who " adopts " a private of the Black Watch and treats him as her son, was on a very high level of histrionic art.

And in the June of 1918, an enthralling little piece called *A Well-remembered Voice* was produced at Wyndham's, in which the ghost of a son killed in the war appeared, asked a thousand things of home, and bade his father take to his pipe again and not be dismal, " for we over here in the dark, you know, have our fun " and " most of us are young, you know." The acting of Sir J. Forbes Robertson as the father in this exquisite little play created an ineffaceable impression, while the gentle but very telling irony in the play at the expense of the crude spiritualism of which we heard so much during the great war reminded the audience that Sir James Barrie is not only one of our most imaginative writers but also one of our sane ones.

The Real Thing at Last, given at the Coliseum in March, 1920, was a comment on Shakespeare on the " Movies," showing a

film version of " Macbeth " which had been
" released " from an iron cage. The film was
presented to an absurd pianoforte accom-
paniment with the usual " letters " and
" captions " on the screen. One of the
" letters " ran as follows :—

> Dear Macbeth, The King has gotten old and silly.
> Slay him.—Yours sincerely, LADY M.

Among the " captions " were : " The
Drawing-room at the Macbeths : the Soliloquy of the King, ' Those Macbeths : I
don't trust them ' " ; " One murder begets
another, so is the whole world kin " ; and
" A Happy Ending : Macduff Forgives
and Forgets." As a finale, Macbeth and
Lady Macbeth are reunited and live happy
ever after. And in *The Truth about the
Russian Dancers*, produced at the Coliseum
in March, 1920, we had an amusing picture
of life as lived in a Russian Ballet, with
Mlle. Tamara Karsavina dancing her way
through the various duties of the day, and
Mr. C. M. Lowne, the original Kit Upjohn
in *Walker, London,* showing once more
what an amusing comedian he can be.

But of all our author's short plays, by far
the most serious was that called *Der Tag*,
produced at the Coliseum in December,

1914, when the English nation was still aflame with rage at the German invasion of Belgium and the destruction wrought in the city of Louvain, and when the exhibition of the photograph of the Belgian King on the screen of this place of entertainment evoked nightly a roar of cheering from the audience, all upstanding to the tune of the " Brabançonne."   This piece presented the German Emperor and his Imperial Chancellor conversing together before the signing of the Declaration of War, and again after the invasion of Belgium. In the opening scene between the All Highest and the Chancellor, we have the following :—

CHANCELLOR (*suavely*) : Your Imperial Majesty, Britain will not join in just now.

EMPEROR : If I was sure of that !

CHANCELLOR : I vouch for it. So well have we chosen our time it finds Britain at issue with herself, her wild women let loose, her Colonies ready to turn against her, Ireland aflame, and the contemptible British Army sulking with the civic powers.

EMPEROR : These wounds might heal suddenly if German bugles sounded. It is a land that in the past has done things.

AN OFFICER : In the past, your Imperial Majesty ; but in the past alone lies Britain's greatness. . . .

CHANCELLOR : How well you know her, Sire.

Then in a dream his Majesty is visited by the Spirit of Culture. There is yet time for the Emperor to save his people and the world, for the declaration of war is as yet unsigned, and this wiser counsellor gives him a warning :—

> One last word to you at the parting of the ways. France, Russia, Britain, these are great opponents, but it is not they who will bring the pillars of Germany down. Beware of Belgium !

Later she visits him again. The war is now supposed to be nearing its end, France and England are drawing ever nearer to a Germany now peopled with little more than ghosts, and the wretched Emperor can only whimper, " I thought England was grown degenerate and would not fight." To which the Shade replies :—

> England has fought you where Crecy was, and Agincourt and Waterloo, with all their dead to help her. The dead became quick in their ancient graves, stirred by the tread of the island feet, and they cried out, " How is England doing ? " And the living answered the dead upon their bugles with the " All's Well." England, O Emperor, *was* grown degenerate, but you have made her great again.

Finally the desperate man cries, " But Germany ? God cannot let my Germany

be utterly destroyed !" And the last words
of the Spirit of Culture are: "If God is
with the Allies, Germany will not be destroyed.   Farewell !" This fine fragment of
history in the form of a play was rather
derided by some of the critics, who took the
lofty attitude of treating it as Propaganda
and therefore not Art. I submit with all
respect that they were mistaken in
allowing this rather academic scruple to out-
weigh the patriotism they all felt and did
so much to fan in a thousand ways.   In all
the countries engaged in that terrible conflict
great literature was directly inspired by it,
and to dismiss it scornfully as Propaganda
would be to perpetrate a deplorable injus-
tice.   Long after the exciting circumstances
of its production and the fine acting in it of
Mr. Norman McKinnel and Miss Irene Vanbrugh are forgotten, this short drama will
be remembered if only for its thrilling
sentence, "Beware of Belgium !" Never
were three words in a play more crammed
with moral import and historical truth.
In the moment of the first German soldier
setting his foot on Belgian soil, Germany
lost the war.

Epilogue.

So we arrive at the end of our record—
though fortunately not at the end of
our dramatist's. It must be the hope of
every British playgoer that many and
many an audience has yet to experience
the enchantments of a Barrie first night;
and with two such later plays before
us as *Dear Brutus* and *Mary Rose*, our gratitude may well be a lively sense of favours
to come. The British stage has not often
stood in greater need than to-day of the
notes of sweetness and wisdom, daintiness
and imagination, which Sir J. M. Barrie
has fashioned so often into beautiful tunes.

This history, so far as it has gone, has
exhibited not only a unique talent but an
extraordinarily consistent one. Over a

period of more than thirty years we have
seen it at work, and how few have been its
failures, how many and how brilliant its
successes ! There must have been a rare
freshness in that first piece of his, the Ibsen
burlesque, for a writer like the present
scribe, who does not recall seeing it more
than once and who had no knowledge of
any sort of the author at the time, to remember the aspects and tones of its players,
and more than one passage of its dialogue.
As long as I live, too, I shall remember the
first occasion of my seeing *Peter Pan*, standing at the back of the packed pit in the Duke
of York's Theatre. (I may add, in paren-
thesis, that I also vividly recall the last time
I saw it at that theatre. I had taken a small
friend who was paying it her first visit, and
at the end of the third Act, when the lights
of the theatre had brightened, she sat
looking up at me with her grey eyes wide
open and full of sad reproach. " Oh—h—h ! "
she said, in an awe-stricken whisper, " *you
have been asleep !* " I could only falter,
" I know I have, my dear, but this is the
thirteenth time I have seen it." May I
be permitted also to add, in mere self-
defence, that since then I have seen it

several times more without deplorably
earning such a rebuke.)

In the Prologue to this book I have
referred to the early ties between our
author and George Meredith, Robert Louis
Stevenson, W. E. Henley, and Sir W. Robertson Nicoll; and here, in its Epilogue, it
is pleasant to record that when, in May,
1922, he delivered his Rectorial address
at St. Andrews he made eloquent reference
in it to the first three as men not of genius
only but of courage, and had the pleasure
of conferring an honorary degree upon the
fourth. Sir J. M. Barrie's address on this
occasion was surely the least academic
and probably the most inspiring ever delivered on such an occasion. It took an
hour and a half to deliver, and the report of
it occupied a whole page of the *Times*
newspaper. A week or two before, he had
warned a friend that he was preparing a
speech for St. Andrews that would be " as
long as a two-act play." It proved to be
not only as long but as interesting as the
best two-act play ever written. Next day
he was presented with the Freedom of the
city, and on this occasion the Provost of
the city, the Rev. A. D. Sloan, said of him

that he had called into existence and perfected a form of dramatic art peculiarly his own, in which the characters born of his imagination moved through the unrelated fancies of a dream ; and added : " The creation of *Peter Pan* was an achievement which in itself has assigned him a permanent place in the Valhalla of literary art." It was on this occasion also that Miss Ellen Terry received an honorary degree, and here are the words in which the Rector alluded to the new *alumna* of St. Andrews :

> The loveliest of all young actresses, the dearest of all old ones—it seems only yesterday that all the men of imagination proposed to their beloveds in some such frenzied words as these : " As I can't get Miss Terry, may I have you ?"

Later in the day he and his Alice Grey, of *Alice Sit-by-the-Fire*, were photographed together in cap and gown, and a very pretty picture they made ; and at night, when three hundred students serenaded him by torchlight, one of the songs with which they regaled him was the Pirates' chorus from *Peter Pan*.

I suppose Sir J. M. Barrie's most brilliant

period of authorship was that which witnessed the production, within virtually two years, of *The Admirable Crichton, Quality Street, Little Mary,* and *Peter Pan,* though even that was almost equalled twelve and more years later, by the production in succession of *A Kiss for Cinderella, Dear Brutus* (both of these written during the great war) and *Mary Rose.* As to the variousness of his work, one need only mention the sheer jolliness of *Walker, London,* the genuine romance of *The Little Minister,* the searching irony of *The Admirable Crichton,* the old-world fragrance and sweetness of *Quality Street,* the brilliant constructive quality of the second Act of *Alice Sit-by-the-Fire,* the manly tenderness of the chief scene in *Dear Brutus,* and the almost unendurable pathos of the last Act of *Mary Rose.* When we add to all this the juvenile fantasy of *Peter Pan* it does indeed become difficult to think of any other modern dramatist, British or foreign, who has combined such variety of theme with such unity of quality.

We have seen how the novelist who so wrung his readers' hearts in pages of " A Window in Thrums " and " Tommy and

Grizel," has produced exactly the same effect in a playhouse ; how the love and tenderness with which his " Margaret Ogilvie " is charged, have been breathed again and again into his dramatic writings, and how the fun which so often enriches his books abounds in his comic writings for the stage.   Referring to his friend, Charles Frohman, he once said : " I wanted to go on writing novels—he wanted me to go on writing plays."   All things considered, Charles Frohman's advice was, I think, the right one.   His plays have had a longer life than most novels enjoy, and countless thousands of people have seen them.   He has, however, founded no school.   He has remained from the first a unique figure of our stage.   As the ghost in " Cymbeline " cries—

> In Britain where was he
> That could stand up his parallel ?

Unlike Lord Dundreary's swallow, he has flocked by himself and made a summer.

One muses gratefully too upon the accomplished actors and actresses who have interpreted him.   On this subject I ventured to ask my friend, Mr. Richard Dickins, one of the most experienced of playgoers, and, as a true *amateur* of culture, one of the best of critics, to favour me with his views, and he has been so good as to send me the following very interesting

STRAY THOUGHTS ON BARRIE ACTORS.

Few, if any, dramatic authors owe as much to the producers of their plays and to those who have acted in them as does Sir J. M. Barrie. From *Walker, London*, in 1892, to *Mary Rose* in 1920, the original production of each play has been well-nigh perfect, and in several cases, notably in *The Admirable Crichton* and *Rosalind*, the acting throughout has been extraordinarily fine.

Most of our leading actors and actresses, from the incomparable Ellen Terry downwards, have at one time or another appeared under the Barrie banner, but there are some half-dozen artists whom the Author's enthusiastic followers especially associate with his plays.

Gerald du Maurier has, since 1902, acted the Hon. Ernest Woolley, Mr. Darling, James Hook, Lord Rolfe, Pantaloon, John Shand, The Policeman (in *A Kiss for Cinderella*), and Dearth (in *Dear Brutus*). Moreover, *What Every Woman Knows*, *A Kiss for Cinderella* and *Dear Brutus* were produced under his management and direction.

Since 1892, Irene Vanbrugh has appeared as Bell Golightly, Amy Grey, Kate, Lady Mary Lasenby, Rosalind, Lady Lillian Garson, and the Spirit of Culture (in *Der Tag*). Hilda

Trevelyan made an instant success as Wendy on the production of *Peter Pan* in 1904, and followed it by appearing as Richardson, Maggie Wylie, Miss Thing (in *A Kiss for Cinderella*), and Patty (in the revival of *Quality Street* at the Haymarket in 1921). Nina Boucicault was the original and only perfect Peter Pan : her performance of this part has never been approached. She was also the original Moira Looney in *Little Mary*, and acted Susan Throssell when *Quality Street* was revived at the Vaudeville in 1913.

The late H. B. Irving was the Paul Digby of *The Wedding Guest* in 1900, and as Bill Crichton, in 1902, made what may almost be described as the artistic success of his life. Barrie lovers who saw that performance will never forget it. Neither will they cease to remember the exquisite embodiment of the sisters Susan and Phœbe Throssell by Marion Terry and Ellaline Terriss when *Quality Street* was produced in 1902.

There is also Winifred Fraser, less well remembered, not so much because the memory of the average theatre-goer does not extend over many years, as because her principal opportunities for distinction as a Barrie actress occurred after she had left England. After acting Moira Looney at Wyndham's, in 1903, Miss Fraser was engaged by Robert Brough and created the parts of Moira and Phœbe Throssell in Australia. Later she settled in New York, and her American appellation of

" The Greatest Stage Mother " is due in no
small extent to her acting in *The New Word*
and, still more, to her delicacy and charm
as Mrs. Morland in *Mary Rose*.

To these recollections I would once again
add my own grateful tribute to Mr. George
Shelton for his Tesman, Ben, and Smee,
all unsurpassable in their neatness and
drollery ; to the memory of the late Mr.
Robb Harwood for his superb Captain of
the Pirates ; to Mr. Edmund Gwenn for his
Sir Harry Sim in *The Twelve Pound Look*,
and to Miss Mary Barton for her original
performance of that gentleman's second
wife, which came gratefully back to memory
when I saw her once more in 1922 as Miss
Willoughby in the Haymarket Theatre
revival of *Quality Street*.

So, with all these and many more happy
memories crowding upon us, we bid the
Master who made them Good-night! but not
Good-bye !

> . . . . The full-blown flower
> Of all the year—this evening hour—
>   With friendship's flame is bright ;
> Life still is sweet, the heavens are fair,
> Though fields are brown and woods are bare,
> And many a joy is left to share
>   Before we say good-night !

What Dr. Oliver Wendell Holmes says here so prettily about " friendship's flame " may surely with very little alteration be applied to the relationship between grateful playgoers on the one side and a beloved dramatist and his interpreters on the other. It is no fragile tie that binds these together, and least of all is it so in England, this dear land of faithful hearts.

Bibliography.

" Letters of George Meredith." (Constable & Co.).
 1912.

" Letters of Robert Louis Stevenson." (Methuen &
 Co.). 1911.

" Charles Frohman, Manager and Man." By J. F.
 Marcosson and D. Frohman. (John Lane). 1916.

" The Plays óf J. M. Barrie." (Hodder & Stoughton).
 1914, etc.

" Walker, London." By J. M. Barrie. (Samuel
 French). 1907.

" Der Tag." By J. M. Barrie. (Hodder & Stoughton).
 1914.

" Jane Annie." By J. M. Barrie and A. Conan Doyle.
 (Chappell & Co.). 1893.

 The Fortnightly Review. (December, 1900).

Index.

"My humble branch of literature may be described as playing hide-and-seek with angels. My puppets seem more real to me than myself."

— From Sir J. M. Barrie's Rectorial Addres
at St. Andrews : May, 1922.